50 Party Appetizer Food Recipes for Home

By: Kelly Johnson

Table of Contents

- Mini Caprese Skewers
- Bacon-Wrapped Dates
- Spinach Artichoke Dip
- Stuffed Mushrooms
- Chicken Satay with Peanut Sauce
- Bruschetta
- Deviled Eggs
- Shrimp Cocktail
- Mini Quiche
- Meatballs in Marinara Sauce
- Spanakopita Triangles
- Jalapeno Poppers
- Crab Cakes
- Antipasto Skewers
- Garlic Parmesan Chicken Wings
- Cucumber Canapés
- Pigs in a Blanket
- Smoked Salmon Crostini
- Buffalo Cauliflower Bites
- Mozzarella Sticks
- Greek Salad Skewers
- Sushi Rolls
- Prosciutto-Wrapped Asparagus
- Chicken Empanadas
- Sweet Potato Fries
- Cheese-Stuffed Mini Bell Peppers
- Falafel Balls
- Stuffed Cherry Tomatoes
- Beef Sliders
- Crab Rangoon
- Mini Tacos
- Onion Rings
- BBQ Chicken Skewers
- Fried Calamari
- Artichoke Dip Stuffed Bread
- Spring Rolls

- Loaded Potato Skins
- Avocado Toast Bites
- Bruschetta with Fig and Goat Cheese
- Baked Brie with Jam
- Teriyaki Beef Skewers
- Chicken Quesadillas
- Greek Spanakopita
- Tomato Basil Crostini
- Coconut Shrimp
- Pesto Pinwheels
- Crab-Stuffed Mushrooms
- Mini Beef Wellingtons
- Stuffed Jalapeno Peppers
- Mediterranean Hummus Platter

Mini Caprese Skewers

Ingredients:

- Fresh cherry or grape tomatoes
- Fresh mini mozzarella balls (bocconcini)
- Fresh basil leaves
- Balsamic glaze or balsamic vinegar (optional)
- Extra virgin olive oil
- Salt and pepper, to taste
- Toothpicks or small skewers

Instructions:

1. **Prepare Ingredients:**
   - Wash the cherry tomatoes and basil leaves. Pat them dry with paper towels.
   - Drain the mini mozzarella balls if they were stored in liquid.
2. **Assemble Skewers:**
   - Take a toothpick or small skewer and thread on one cherry tomato.
   - Follow with a basil leaf folded or rolled up slightly.
   - Next, thread on a mini mozzarella ball.
   - Repeat the sequence until the skewer is filled, ending with a cherry tomato.
3. **Arrange and Season:**
   - Place the assembled skewers on a serving platter or dish.
   - Drizzle with a little extra virgin olive oil.
   - Optionally, drizzle with balsamic glaze or vinegar for added flavor.
   - Season lightly with salt and pepper to taste.
4. **Serve:**
   - Arrange the Mini Caprese Skewers neatly on a platter.
   - Serve immediately or refrigerate until ready to serve.

Tips:

- Choose ripe and flavorful cherry tomatoes for the best taste.
- If using wooden skewers, soak them in water for about 30 minutes before assembling to prevent them from burning.
- You can customize these skewers by adding a twist, such as a slice of prosciutto or a sprinkle of Italian seasoning.
- These skewers are best served fresh but can be refrigerated for a few hours before serving. If making ahead, drizzle with the olive oil just before serving to keep them fresh.

Enjoy these Mini Caprese Skewers as a tasty and elegant appetizer at your next gathering!

Bacon-Wrapped Dates

Ingredients:

- Medjool dates, pitted (about 24 dates)
- Thinly sliced bacon, cut into halves (12 slices)
- Optional: Whole almonds or pistachios, toasted

Instructions:

1. **Preheat Oven:**
   - Preheat your oven to 375°F (190°C). Line a baking sheet with parchment paper or foil for easy cleanup.
2. **Prepare Dates:**
   - If your dates have pits, carefully slit each date lengthwise and remove the pit.
   - Optionally, stuff each date with a toasted almond or pistachio for added crunch and flavor.
3. **Wrap with Bacon:**
   - Take a half-slice of bacon and wrap it around each date. Secure the bacon with a toothpick if necessary.
4. **Arrange on Baking Sheet:**
   - Place the bacon-wrapped dates on the prepared baking sheet, seam side down.
5. **Bake:**
   - Bake in the preheated oven for 15-20 minutes, or until the bacon is crispy and cooked to your liking.
6. **Serve:**
   - Remove from the oven and let cool slightly before serving.
   - Serve warm as is or with a dipping sauce of your choice (e.g., balsamic glaze, honey mustard).

Tips:

- Use Medjool dates for their sweetness and larger size, which pairs well with the salty bacon.
- If the bacon isn't crisping up enough, you can broil the dates for the last 1-2 minutes, watching carefully to prevent burning.
- Experiment with different variations by adding a sprinkle of brown sugar or a dash of cayenne pepper for a sweet and spicy twist.
- These bacon-wrapped dates can be made ahead of time and reheated in the oven before serving. They're sure to be a hit at any party or gathering!

Spinach Artichoke Dip

Ingredients:

- 1 (10 oz) package frozen chopped spinach, thawed and drained
- 1 (14 oz) can artichoke hearts, drained and chopped
- 1 cup grated Parmesan cheese
- 1 cup shredded mozzarella cheese
- 1 cup mayonnaise
- 1 cup sour cream
- 2 cloves garlic, minced
- 1/2 teaspoon salt
- 1/4 teaspoon black pepper
- Optional: Dash of cayenne pepper or red pepper flakes for a bit of heat
- Optional: Additional grated Parmesan cheese for topping

Instructions:

1. **Preheat Oven:**
   - Preheat your oven to 350°F (175°C).
2. **Prepare Spinach and Artichokes:**
   - Thaw the frozen chopped spinach and drain well to remove excess water.
   - Drain and chop the artichoke hearts into small pieces.
3. **Mix Ingredients:**
   - In a large mixing bowl, combine the drained spinach, chopped artichoke hearts, grated Parmesan cheese, shredded mozzarella cheese, mayonnaise, sour cream, minced garlic, salt, black pepper, and optional cayenne pepper or red pepper flakes. Mix until well combined.
4. **Bake:**
   - Transfer the mixture to a baking dish (an 8x8 inch dish or similar size works well). Smooth out the top with a spatula.
   - Sprinkle additional grated Parmesan cheese on top, if desired.
5. **Bake:**
   - Bake in the preheated oven for 25-30 minutes, or until the dip is hot and bubbly around the edges and the top is golden brown.
6. **Serve:**
   - Remove from the oven and let it cool for a few minutes before serving.
   - Serve warm with tortilla chips, crackers, sliced baguette, or vegetable sticks for dipping.

Tips:

- Make sure to thoroughly drain the spinach to avoid excess water in the dip, which can make it too watery.

- You can adjust the amount of garlic and seasonings to suit your taste preferences.
- This dip can also be made ahead of time and stored in the refrigerator until ready to bake. Simply cover tightly with plastic wrap or foil before refrigerating.
- Leftovers can be stored in an airtight container in the refrigerator for a few days and reheated in the microwave or oven.

Enjoy this creamy and delicious Spinach Artichoke Dip as a crowd-pleasing appetizer at your next gathering!

Stuffed Mushrooms

Ingredients:

- 24 large white or cremini mushrooms
- 1 tablespoon olive oil
- 2 cloves garlic, minced
- 1/2 cup finely chopped onion
- 1/2 cup finely chopped bell pepper (any color)
- 1/2 cup breadcrumbs (plain or seasoned)
- 1/2 cup grated Parmesan cheese
- 1/4 cup chopped fresh parsley
- Salt and pepper, to taste
- Optional: 1/4 teaspoon red pepper flakes for a bit of heat
- Optional: 1/4 cup chopped sun-dried tomatoes or cooked crumbled sausage

Instructions:

1. **Preheat Oven:**
    - Preheat your oven to 375°F (190°C). Line a baking sheet with parchment paper or foil.
2. **Prepare Mushrooms:**
    - Gently wipe the mushrooms clean with a damp cloth or paper towel to remove any dirt. Remove the stems from the mushrooms and finely chop them. Set the mushroom caps aside.
3. **Prepare Filling:**
    - In a large skillet, heat olive oil over medium heat. Add the minced garlic and chopped onion, sautéing until softened and fragrant, about 3-4 minutes.
    - Add the chopped mushroom stems and bell pepper to the skillet. Cook for another 5-6 minutes until the mushrooms are tender and any liquid has evaporated.
    - Remove from heat and stir in the breadcrumbs, Parmesan cheese, chopped parsley, salt, pepper, and optional red pepper flakes. If using sun-dried tomatoes or cooked sausage, add them to the mixture as well.
4. **Stuff the Mushrooms:**
    - Spoon the filling mixture generously into each mushroom cap, mounding it slightly.
5. **Bake:**
    - Arrange the stuffed mushrooms on the prepared baking sheet.
    - Bake in the preheated oven for 20-25 minutes, or until the mushrooms are tender and the tops are golden brown.
6. **Serve:**
    - Remove from the oven and let cool slightly before serving.
    - Serve warm as an appetizer or party snack.

Tips:

- Choose mushrooms that are uniform in size for even cooking.
- You can prepare the filling ahead of time and refrigerate it until ready to use. Stuff the mushrooms just before baking.
- Experiment with different variations by adding ingredients like bacon, spinach, cream cheese, or different herbs and spices.
- Leftover stuffed mushrooms can be stored in an airtight container in the refrigerator for a couple of days. Reheat in the oven or microwave before serving.

Enjoy these delicious stuffed mushrooms at your next gathering or as a tasty appetizer!

Chicken Satay with Peanut Sauce

Chicken Satay Ingredients:

- 1 lb (450g) boneless, skinless chicken breasts or thighs, cut into thin strips
- Wooden skewers, soaked in water for at least 30 minutes

Marinade Ingredients:

- 1/4 cup coconut milk
- 2 tablespoons soy sauce
- 2 tablespoons fish sauce
- 2 tablespoons brown sugar
- 1 tablespoon curry powder
- 1 teaspoon turmeric powder
- 2 cloves garlic, minced
- 1 tablespoon vegetable oil

Peanut Sauce Ingredients:

- 1/2 cup creamy peanut butter
- 1/4 cup coconut milk
- 2 tablespoons soy sauce
- 2 tablespoons brown sugar
- 1 tablespoon lime juice
- 1 teaspoon sesame oil
- 1 clove garlic, minced
- 1/2 teaspoon grated fresh ginger
- Water (as needed to thin the sauce)

Instructions:

1. **Prepare Chicken:**
   - In a bowl, combine all the marinade ingredients: coconut milk, soy sauce, fish sauce, brown sugar, curry powder, turmeric powder, minced garlic, and vegetable oil. Mix well.
   - Add the chicken strips to the marinade, making sure they are well coated. Cover and refrigerate for at least 30 minutes, or up to 4 hours.
2. **Make Peanut Sauce:**
   - In a small saucepan over medium-low heat, combine peanut butter, coconut milk, soy sauce, brown sugar, lime juice, sesame oil, minced garlic, and grated ginger.
   - Stir continuously until the peanut butter melts and the sauce is smooth. If the sauce is too thick, gradually add water (1 tablespoon at a time) until you reach the desired consistency. Remove from heat and set aside.

3. **Skewer Chicken:**
    - Preheat your grill or grill pan over medium-high heat.
    - Thread the marinated chicken strips onto the soaked wooden skewers, dividing them evenly among the skewers.
4. **Grill Chicken Satay:**
    - Grill the chicken skewers for about 3-4 minutes per side, or until fully cooked and slightly charred. Cooking time may vary depending on the thickness of the chicken strips.
5. **Serve:**
    - Arrange the grilled Chicken Satay skewers on a platter.
    - Serve immediately with the prepared Peanut Sauce on the side for dipping.

Tips:

- If using bamboo skewers, remember to soak them in water for at least 30 minutes before threading the chicken to prevent them from burning on the grill.
- Feel free to adjust the seasoning and spice level of the marinade and peanut sauce according to your taste preferences.
- Chicken Satay and Peanut Sauce can also be served with a side of cucumber salad or steamed rice for a complete meal.
- Leftover Peanut Sauce can be stored in an airtight container in the refrigerator for up to a week. Heat gently before serving again.

Enjoy this flavorful Chicken Satay with Peanut Sauce as a delicious appetizer or main dish at your next gathering!

Bruschetta

Ingredients:

- 1 French baguette or Italian loaf, sliced into 1/2-inch thick slices
- 4-5 ripe tomatoes, diced
- 2 cloves garlic, minced
- 6-8 fresh basil leaves, chiffonade (thinly sliced)
- 2 tablespoons extra virgin olive oil
- 1 tablespoon balsamic vinegar (optional)
- Salt and freshly ground black pepper, to taste

Instructions:

1. **Prepare Bread:**
    - Preheat your oven to 400°F (200°C).
    - Arrange the bread slices on a baking sheet in a single layer. Brush both sides lightly with olive oil.
    - Bake in the preheated oven for about 5-7 minutes, flipping halfway through, until the bread slices are golden and crispy. Remove from oven and let cool slightly.
2. **Prepare Tomato Mixture:**
    - In a mixing bowl, combine the diced tomatoes, minced garlic, chiffonade basil leaves, extra virgin olive oil, and balsamic vinegar (if using).
    - Season with salt and pepper to taste. Toss gently to combine all the ingredients.
3. **Assemble Bruschetta:**
    - Spoon a generous amount of the tomato mixture onto each toasted bread slice.
    - Drizzle a little more olive oil and balsamic vinegar on top, if desired, for extra flavor.
4. **Serve:**
    - Arrange the Tomato Bruschetta on a serving platter.
    - Serve immediately as an appetizer or starter.

Tips:

- For extra flavor, rub the toasted bread slices with a cut clove of garlic before topping with the tomato mixture.
- You can customize your Bruschetta by adding toppings such as fresh mozzarella slices, chopped olives, or a sprinkle of grated Parmesan cheese.
- Make sure to use ripe and flavorful tomatoes for the best taste.

Enjoy this simple and delicious Tomato Bruschetta as a fresh and vibrant appetizer for any occasion!

Deviled Eggs

Ingredients:

- 6 large eggs
- 3 tablespoons mayonnaise
- 1 teaspoon Dijon mustard
- 1/2 teaspoon white vinegar
- Salt and pepper, to taste
- Paprika or chopped fresh parsley, for garnish

Instructions:

1. **Hard Boil Eggs:**
   - Place the eggs in a saucepan and cover with cold water. Bring to a boil over medium-high heat.
   - Once boiling, cover the saucepan with a lid and remove from heat. Let the eggs sit in the hot water for 10-12 minutes.
   - Drain the hot water and transfer the eggs to a bowl of ice water to cool for a few minutes.
2. **Prepare Eggs:**
   - Once cooled, peel the eggs under cool running water. Gently tap each egg on a hard surface and carefully peel away the shell.
3. **Cut and Scoop Out Yolks:**
   - Slice each egg in half lengthwise. Carefully remove the yolks and place them in a separate bowl.
   - Arrange the egg white halves on a serving platter.
4. **Make Filling:**
   - Mash the egg yolks with a fork until smooth and no large lumps remain.
   - Add mayonnaise, Dijon mustard, white vinegar, salt, and pepper to the mashed yolks. Mix well until creamy and combined.
5. **Fill Egg Whites:**
   - Spoon or pipe the yolk mixture evenly into the hollowed-out egg white halves.
6. **Garnish and Serve:**
   - Sprinkle the filled deviled eggs with paprika or chopped fresh parsley for garnish.
   - Serve immediately or cover and refrigerate until ready to serve.

Tips:

- To pipe the yolk mixture neatly into the egg whites, you can use a piping bag fitted with a star tip or simply snip off the corner of a resealable plastic bag.
- Experiment with additional ingredients such as chopped chives, diced pickles, or a dash of hot sauce to customize the flavor of your deviled eggs.

- Deviled eggs can be made ahead of time and stored in the refrigerator. Keep them covered with plastic wrap or in an airtight container until ready to serve.

Enjoy these creamy and flavorful Deviled Eggs as a classic appetizer that's always a crowd-pleaser!

Shrimp Cocktail

Ingredients:

For the Shrimp:

- 1 lb (about 450g) large shrimp, peeled and deveined, tails left on
- 1 lemon, sliced
- 2 bay leaves
- Salt

For the Cocktail Sauce:

- 1/2 cup ketchup
- 2 tablespoons prepared horseradish (adjust to taste)
- 1 tablespoon lemon juice
- 1 teaspoon Worcestershire sauce
- Dash of hot sauce (optional)
- Salt and pepper, to taste

For Serving:

- Fresh lemon wedges
- Fresh parsley, chopped (optional)
- Ice, for serving

Instructions:

1. **Prepare the Shrimp:**
    - In a large pot, fill with water and add sliced lemon, bay leaves, and a generous pinch of salt.
    - Bring the water to a boil over medium-high heat.
    - Add the shrimp to the boiling water and cook for 2-3 minutes, or until the shrimp are pink and opaque.
    - Remove the shrimp from the water and immediately transfer to a bowl of ice water to stop the cooking process.
    - Once cooled, drain the shrimp and pat dry with paper towels. Chill in the refrigerator until ready to serve.
2. **Make Cocktail Sauce:**
    - In a small bowl, combine ketchup, prepared horseradish, lemon juice, Worcestershire sauce, hot sauce (if using), salt, and pepper. Adjust the amount of horseradish to your taste preference for spiciness.
3. **Serve Shrimp Cocktail:**
    - Arrange the chilled shrimp on a serving platter or individual cocktail glasses lined with ice.

- Place a small bowl of cocktail sauce in the center of the platter or glasses.
- Garnish with lemon wedges and chopped fresh parsley, if desired.

Tips:

- Ensure the shrimp are fully cooled before serving to maintain their texture and firmness.
- To devein the shrimp, make a shallow cut along the back of each shrimp with a paring knife and remove the dark vein with the tip of the knife or a small spoon.
- For an extra touch, you can add a splash of vodka or a squeeze of additional lemon juice to the cocktail sauce.
- Shrimp Cocktail is best served immediately after assembling, while the shrimp are cold and the sauce is fresh.

Enjoy this classic and elegant Shrimp Cocktail as a refreshing appetizer for any occasion!

Mini Quiche

Ingredients:

For the Quiche Filling:

- 4 large eggs
- 1/2 cup milk or heavy cream
- Salt and pepper, to taste
- 1/2 cup shredded cheese (such as cheddar, Swiss, or Gruyere)
- Fillings of your choice (e.g., cooked bacon or ham, sautéed vegetables like spinach, mushrooms, bell peppers, etc.)

For the Crust (optional):

- 1 sheet of puff pastry or pie crust, thawed if frozen

Instructions:

1. **Preheat Oven:**
   - Preheat your oven to 375°F (190°C). Grease a mini muffin tin or line with paper liners for easier removal.
2. **Prepare Crust (if using):**
   - If using puff pastry or pie crust, roll out the dough on a lightly floured surface. Using a round cookie cutter or rim of a glass, cut out circles slightly larger than the mini muffin tin cavities.
   - Press each circle gently into the bottom and sides of the muffin tin cavities to form mini tart shells.
3. **Prepare Quiche Filling:**
   - In a mixing bowl, whisk together eggs, milk or cream, salt, and pepper until well combined.
   - Stir in shredded cheese and your chosen fillings (previously cooked and cooled if necessary).
4. **Assemble Mini Quiches:**
   - Spoon the quiche filling mixture into each mini tart shell, filling nearly to the top.
5. **Bake:**
   - Bake in the preheated oven for 15-20 minutes, or until the quiches are puffed and the edges are golden brown. The filling should be set and slightly firm to the touch.
6. **Serve:**
   - Remove the mini quiches from the muffin tin and let them cool on a wire rack for a few minutes before serving.
   - Serve warm as an appetizer or light meal.

Tips:

- Customize your mini quiches by using different combinations of fillings such as spinach and feta, bacon and cheddar, or mushroom and Swiss cheese.
- If you prefer a crustless version, simply grease the mini muffin tin well and pour the quiche filling directly into each cavity.
- Mini quiches can be made ahead of time and stored in the refrigerator. Reheat in the oven before serving to maintain their crispiness.
- Garnish with fresh herbs like chopped chives or parsley before serving for added flavor and presentation.

Enjoy these Mini Quiches as a delicious and versatile appetizer that will impress your guests!

Meatballs in Marinara Sauce

Ingredients:

For the Meatballs:

- 1 lb (450g) ground beef (you can also use a mix of beef and pork)
- 1/2 cup breadcrumbs
- 1/4 cup grated Parmesan cheese
- 1/4 cup milk
- 1 egg
- 2 cloves garlic, minced
- 1 tablespoon fresh parsley, finely chopped
- 1 teaspoon dried oregano
- 1/2 teaspoon salt
- 1/4 teaspoon black pepper
- Olive oil, for cooking

For the Marinara Sauce:

- 1 (28 oz) can crushed tomatoes
- 1 small onion, finely chopped
- 2 cloves garlic, minced
- 1 teaspoon dried basil
- 1 teaspoon dried oregano
- 1/2 teaspoon dried thyme
- 1/2 teaspoon red pepper flakes (optional, for heat)
- Salt and pepper, to taste
- Fresh basil leaves, chopped (for garnish)

Instructions:

1. **Make the Meatballs:**
   - In a large mixing bowl, combine ground beef, breadcrumbs, grated Parmesan cheese, milk, egg, minced garlic, chopped parsley, dried oregano, salt, and black pepper.
   - Mix well until all ingredients are evenly combined.
   - Shape the mixture into meatballs, about 1 to 1.5 inches in diameter.
2. **Cook the Meatballs:**
   - Heat olive oil in a large skillet over medium-high heat.
   - Add the meatballs in batches, making sure not to overcrowd the pan. Cook until browned on all sides, about 6-8 minutes. Transfer the browned meatballs to a plate lined with paper towels to drain excess oil.
3. **Make the Marinara Sauce:**

- In the same skillet, add a little more olive oil if needed. Sauté the chopped onion until softened and translucent, about 3-4 minutes.
- Add minced garlic, dried basil, dried oregano, dried thyme, and red pepper flakes (if using). Cook for another minute until fragrant.
- Pour in the crushed tomatoes and season with salt and pepper to taste. Stir to combine.
- Bring the sauce to a simmer. Reduce the heat to low and let it simmer gently for about 15-20 minutes, stirring occasionally, to allow the flavors to meld together.

4. **Combine and Simmer:**
   - Carefully add the cooked meatballs back into the skillet with the marinara sauce.
   - Spoon some of the sauce over the meatballs to coat them evenly.
   - Cover the skillet with a lid and simmer on low heat for an additional 15-20 minutes, or until the meatballs are cooked through and the sauce has thickened slightly.
5. **Serve:**
   - Serve the meatballs hot, garnished with chopped fresh basil leaves.
   - They can be served as an appetizer with toothpicks or as a main course over cooked pasta, rice, or with crusty bread.

Tips:

- If you prefer softer meatballs, you can add a few tablespoons of water or chicken broth to the sauce while simmering.
- For a richer sauce, you can stir in a tablespoon or two of tomato paste when adding the crushed tomatoes.
- Leftover meatballs and marinara sauce can be stored in an airtight container in the refrigerator for up to 3-4 days or frozen for longer storage. Reheat gently on the stove or in the microwave before serving.

Enjoy these flavorful Meatballs in Marinara Sauce for a comforting and satisfying meal!

Spanakopita Triangles

Ingredients:

- 1 package (16 oz) frozen chopped spinach, thawed and squeezed dry
- 1 cup crumbled feta cheese
- 1/2 cup ricotta cheese or cottage cheese
- 1/2 cup grated Parmesan cheese
- 3 green onions, finely chopped
- 2 cloves garlic, minced
- 1/4 cup chopped fresh dill (or 1 tablespoon dried dill)
- Salt and pepper, to taste
- 1/4 teaspoon ground nutmeg
- 1/2 cup (1 stick) unsalted butter, melted
- 1 package (16 oz) phyllo dough, thawed according to package instructions
- Olive oil or cooking spray, for brushing

Instructions:

1. **Prepare the Filling:**
   - In a large bowl, combine the thawed and squeezed dry spinach, crumbled feta cheese, ricotta or cottage cheese, grated Parmesan cheese, chopped green onions, minced garlic, chopped fresh dill (or dried dill), salt, pepper, and ground nutmeg. Mix well until evenly combined. Set aside.
2. **Assemble the Spanakopita Triangles:**
   - Preheat your oven to 375°F (190°C). Line a baking sheet with parchment paper.
   - Unroll the phyllo dough sheets on a clean, dry surface. Cover with a damp towel to prevent them from drying out.
   - Take one sheet of phyllo dough and brush it lightly with melted butter. Place another sheet on top and brush with butter again.
   - Cut the buttered phyllo sheets lengthwise into 3 or 4 strips, depending on the desired size of your triangles.
3. **Fill and Fold the Triangles:**
   - Place a spoonful of the spinach and cheese filling at the bottom corner of each strip of phyllo.
   - Fold one corner of the phyllo diagonally across to the opposite edge to form a triangle. Continue folding the triangle along the strip of phyllo until you reach the end.
   - Brush the top of each triangle with more melted butter and place it seam side down on the prepared baking sheet.
   - Repeat with the remaining phyllo sheets and filling until all the triangles are assembled.
4. **Bake the Spanakopita Triangles:**

- Brush the tops of the assembled triangles with a final layer of melted butter or lightly spray with olive oil.
- Bake in the preheated oven for 20-25 minutes, or until the triangles are golden brown and crispy.

5. **Serve:**
   - Remove from the oven and let cool slightly before serving.
   - Spanakopita triangles can be served warm or at room temperature. They are delicious on their own or served with tzatziki sauce or a squeeze of lemon.

Tips:

- Phyllo dough can dry out quickly, so keep it covered with a damp towel while you're working with it.
- If you prefer, you can make larger triangles or even squares by adjusting the size of the phyllo sheets and the amount of filling used.
- Spanakopita triangles can be prepared ahead of time and frozen before baking. Simply arrange them on a baking sheet and freeze until firm, then transfer to a freezer bag or container. Bake directly from frozen, adding a few extra minutes to the baking time.

Enjoy these crispy and flavorful Spanakopita Triangles as a delightful appetizer or snack!

Jalapeno Poppers

Ingredients:

- 12 jalapeño peppers
- 8 oz (225g) cream cheese, softened
- 1 cup shredded cheddar cheese (or cheese of your choice)
- 1/2 teaspoon garlic powder
- 1/2 teaspoon onion powder
- 1/2 teaspoon paprika
- Salt and pepper, to taste
- 1 cup breadcrumbs (plain or seasoned)
- 2 eggs, beaten
- Oil, for frying (if frying)
- Optional: Ranch dressing or sour cream, for serving

Instructions:

1. **Prepare the Jalapeños:**
    - Preheat your oven to 400°F (200°C) if baking, or heat oil in a deep fryer or skillet if frying.
    - Wear gloves to protect your hands from the jalapeño peppers' heat. Slice each jalapeño lengthwise and carefully remove the seeds and membranes with a spoon. Leave the stems intact for easier handling.
2. **Make the Filling:**
    - In a mixing bowl, combine softened cream cheese, shredded cheddar cheese, garlic powder, onion powder, paprika, salt, and pepper. Mix until smooth and well combined.
3. **Stuff the Jalapeños:**
    - Spoon the cheese mixture into each jalapeño half, filling them evenly.
4. **Bread the Jalapeño Poppers:**
    - Place beaten eggs in a shallow bowl and breadcrumbs in another shallow bowl.
    - Dip each stuffed jalapeño half into the beaten eggs, coating evenly.
    - Roll the jalapeños in the breadcrumbs, pressing gently to adhere.
5. **Fry or Bake the Jalapeño Poppers:**
    - **Frying Method:** Heat oil in a deep fryer or large skillet over medium-high heat (about 350°F/175°C). Fry the jalapeño poppers in batches for 2-3 minutes, or until golden brown and crispy. Drain on paper towels.
    - **Baking Method:** Arrange the breaded jalapeño poppers on a baking sheet lined with parchment paper. Bake in the preheated oven for 15-20 minutes, or until the jalapeños are tender and the breadcrumb coating is golden brown and crispy.
6. **Serve:**
    - Remove from the oven or fryer and let cool slightly before serving.

- Serve jalapeño poppers warm as is, or with ranch dressing or sour cream for dipping.

Tips:

- Adjust the spiciness by removing all or some of the jalapeño seeds and membranes. The seeds and membranes contain the most heat.
- If you prefer a lighter version, you can bake the jalapeño poppers instead of frying them.
- To save time, you can prepare the stuffed jalapeños ahead of time and refrigerate them until you're ready to bread and cook them.

Enjoy these delicious Jalapeño Poppers as a spicy and cheesy appetizer that's sure to be a hit at any gathering!

Crab Cakes

Ingredients:

- 1 lb (450g) lump crab meat, picked over for shells
- 1/2 cup breadcrumbs (panko or regular)
- 1/4 cup mayonnaise
- 1 large egg, lightly beaten
- 1 tablespoon Dijon mustard
- 1 tablespoon Worcestershire sauce
- 1 tablespoon lemon juice
- 1/4 cup finely chopped green onions (or chives)
- 2 tablespoons finely chopped parsley
- 1/2 teaspoon Old Bay seasoning (or seafood seasoning)
- Salt and pepper, to taste
- 1/4 cup all-purpose flour (for coating)
- 2-3 tablespoons olive oil or unsalted butter (for frying)
- Lemon wedges, for serving
- Tartar sauce or remoulade, for serving (optional)

Instructions:

1. **Prepare the Crab Cakes:**
    - In a large mixing bowl, gently combine lump crab meat, breadcrumbs, mayonnaise, beaten egg, Dijon mustard, Worcestershire sauce, lemon juice, green onions, parsley, Old Bay seasoning, salt, and pepper. Be careful not to break up the crab meat too much.
2. **Form the Crab Cakes:**
    - Divide the crab mixture into 8 equal portions. Shape each portion into a patty, about 1/2 to 3/4 inch thick. Place the formed crab cakes on a baking sheet lined with parchment paper.
3. **Chill the Crab Cakes (optional):**
    - For best results, cover the baking sheet with plastic wrap and refrigerate the crab cakes for at least 30 minutes to allow them to firm up. Chilling helps the crab cakes hold their shape better during cooking.
4. **Coat and Fry the Crab Cakes:**
    - Heat olive oil or butter in a large skillet over medium heat.
    - Dredge each crab cake in flour, shaking off any excess.
    - Carefully place the crab cakes in the heated skillet and cook for 4-5 minutes per side, or until golden brown and heated through. Add more oil or butter if needed.
    - Transfer the cooked crab cakes to a plate lined with paper towels to drain excess oil.
5. **Serve:**
    - Serve the crab cakes warm, garnished with lemon wedges.

- Optionally, serve with tartar sauce or remoulade on the side for dipping.

Tips:

- Use high-quality lump crab meat for the best texture and flavor in your crab cakes.
- Be gentle when mixing and shaping the crab cakes to keep the crab meat in large chunks.
- If you prefer baked crab cakes, you can place them on a lightly greased baking sheet and bake at 375°F (190°C) for about 12-15 minutes, or until golden brown and heated through.
- Leftover crab cakes can be stored in an airtight container in the refrigerator for up to 2 days. Reheat gently in the oven or skillet before serving.

Enjoy these flavorful Crab Cakes as a delightful appetizer or main dish paired with your favorite sides!

Antipasto Skewers

Ingredients:

- Cherry tomatoes
- Fresh mozzarella balls (bocconcini)
- Slices of salami or prosciutto, folded or rolled up
- Marinated artichoke hearts, drained and halved
- Kalamata olives, pitted
- Basil leaves
- Balsamic glaze (optional), for drizzling

Instructions:

1. **Prepare Ingredients:**
   - If using wooden skewers, soak them in water for about 30 minutes to prevent burning.
   - Prepare the cherry tomatoes, fresh mozzarella balls, salami or prosciutto slices, artichoke hearts, and olives by draining and halving them if necessary.
2. **Assemble Skewers:**
   - Start assembling the skewers by threading on a cherry tomato followed by a folded or rolled slice of salami or prosciutto.
   - Add a fresh mozzarella ball (bocconcini) or a halved marinated artichoke heart.
   - Thread on a Kalamata olive and a basil leaf.
   - Repeat the pattern until the skewer is filled, leaving a little space at the ends for easier handling.
3. **Arrange and Serve:**
   - Place the assembled antipasto skewers on a serving platter or board.
   - If desired, drizzle with balsamic glaze for extra flavor and presentation.
4. **Serve:**
   - Serve the antipasto skewers immediately at room temperature.
   - They can be enjoyed on their own or as part of a larger antipasto platter.

Tips:

- Customize the skewers by adding other antipasto ingredients such as roasted red peppers, marinated cherry peppers, grilled artichoke hearts, or chunks of provolone cheese.
- If making ahead of time, cover the skewers with plastic wrap and refrigerate. Remove from the refrigerator about 15-20 minutes before serving to bring them to room temperature.
- These skewers are versatile and can be adjusted based on personal preferences and dietary restrictions. They're perfect for parties, gatherings, or even as a light snack.

Enjoy these delicious and colorful Antipasto Skewers as a flavorful appetizer that's sure to impress your guests!

Garlic Parmesan Chicken Wings

Ingredients:

For the Chicken Wings:

- 2 lbs (about 1 kg) chicken wings, split into drumettes and flats
- 1 tablespoon baking powder (not baking soda)
- 1/2 teaspoon salt
- 1/2 teaspoon black pepper

For the Garlic Parmesan Sauce:

- 1/4 cup unsalted butter
- 4 cloves garlic, minced
- 1/4 cup grated Parmesan cheese
- 1 tablespoon chopped fresh parsley (optional, for garnish)
- Salt and pepper, to taste

Instructions:

1. **Prepare the Chicken Wings:**
    - Preheat your oven to 425°F (220°C). Line a baking sheet with parchment paper or foil for easy cleanup.
    - Pat the chicken wings dry with paper towels to remove excess moisture.
    - In a bowl, toss the chicken wings with baking powder, salt, and black pepper until evenly coated.
2. **Bake the Chicken Wings:**
    - Arrange the chicken wings in a single layer on the prepared baking sheet, making sure they're not touching each other.
    - Bake in the preheated oven for 40-45 minutes, turning halfway through, until the wings are crispy and golden brown.
3. **Make the Garlic Parmesan Sauce:**
    - In a small saucepan, melt the butter over medium heat.
    - Add the minced garlic and cook for 1-2 minutes until fragrant, stirring constantly.
    - Remove from heat and stir in the grated Parmesan cheese until smooth and well combined. Season with salt and pepper to taste.
4. **Toss the Wings in Sauce:**
    - Transfer the baked chicken wings to a large bowl.
    - Pour the garlic Parmesan sauce over the wings and toss gently until all wings are evenly coated.
5. **Serve:**
    - Transfer the coated wings to a serving platter.
    - Garnish with chopped fresh parsley, if desired, for a pop of color and freshness.

- Serve immediately while hot, optionally with celery sticks and ranch or blue cheese dressing on the side for dipping.

Tips:

- Make sure to use baking powder, not baking soda, as baking powder helps to crisp up the chicken wings.
- For extra crispy wings, you can place the baked wings under the broiler for a couple of minutes after tossing them in the sauce.
- Adjust the amount of garlic and Parmesan cheese in the sauce according to your taste preferences.
- Leftover wings can be stored in an airtight container in the refrigerator for a few days. Reheat in the oven to maintain crispiness before serving.

Enjoy these flavorful Garlic Parmesan Chicken Wings as a delicious appetizer or snack for any occasion!

Cucumber Canapés

Ingredients:

- 1 English cucumber
- 4 oz (about 115g) cream cheese, softened
- 1-2 tablespoons fresh dill, chopped
- 1 teaspoon lemon juice
- Salt and pepper, to taste
- Optional toppings: smoked salmon, cherry tomatoes, sliced olives, fresh herbs (such as chives or parsley), cracked black pepper

Instructions:

1. **Prepare the Cucumber:**
    - Wash the cucumber thoroughly. If desired, peel strips of the cucumber skin lengthwise to create a striped pattern. Slice the cucumber into rounds, about 1/4 to 1/2 inch thick.
2. **Make the Cream Cheese Spread:**
    - In a small bowl, combine the softened cream cheese, chopped fresh dill, lemon juice, salt, and pepper. Mix well until smooth and evenly combined.
3. **Assemble the Cucumber Canapés:**
    - Place the cucumber rounds on a serving platter or tray.
    - Spread a small amount of the cream cheese mixture onto each cucumber round.
4. **Add Toppings (Optional):**
    - Arrange your choice of toppings on top of the cream cheese spread. Some popular options include a small piece of smoked salmon, a halved cherry tomato, a slice of olive, or a sprinkle of fresh herbs and cracked black pepper.
5. **Serve:**
    - Arrange the cucumber canapés neatly on a platter and serve immediately.
    - Alternatively, cover with plastic wrap and refrigerate until ready to serve, but it's best served fresh.

Tips:

- For a variation, you can use flavored cream cheese such as garlic and herb or chive and onion.
- Feel free to experiment with different toppings and combinations to suit your taste preferences or the theme of your event.
- Cucumber canapés are best assembled shortly before serving to keep the cucumbers crisp and fresh.

Enjoy these light and flavorful Cucumber Canapés as a delightful appetizer that will impress your guests!

Pigs in a Blanket

Ingredients:

- 1 package (8 oz) refrigerated crescent roll dough (8 count)
- 24 cocktail sausages (mini hot dogs)
- Mustard or ketchup, for serving (optional)

Instructions:

1. **Preheat the Oven:**
   - Preheat your oven to 375°F (190°C). Line a baking sheet with parchment paper or lightly grease it.
2. **Prepare the Dough:**
   - Unroll the crescent roll dough and separate it into triangles along the perforated lines.
3. **Wrap the Sausages:**
   - Cut each triangle of dough into three smaller triangles by cutting along the existing perforations.
   - Place a cocktail sausage on the wide end of each triangle.
   - Roll up the dough, starting from the wide end, to completely encase the sausage. Repeat with the remaining sausages and dough triangles.
4. **Arrange on Baking Sheet:**
   - Place the wrapped sausages seam-side down on the prepared baking sheet, leaving a little space between each one for even baking.
5. **Bake:**
   - Bake in the preheated oven for 12-15 minutes, or until the dough is golden brown and cooked through.
6. **Serve:**
   - Remove from the oven and let cool for a few minutes before serving.
   - Optionally, serve with mustard or ketchup for dipping.

Tips:

- You can brush the tops of the pigs in a blanket with melted butter before baking to give them a golden finish.
- For variation, you can use puff pastry instead of crescent roll dough for a flakier texture.
- These can be made ahead and stored in the refrigerator. Bake just before serving to ensure they are warm and crispy.

Enjoy these homemade Pigs in a Blanket as a fun and tasty appetizer or snack for any occasion!

Smoked Salmon Crostini

Ingredients:

- 1 French baguette, sliced into 1/2-inch thick rounds
- Olive oil, for brushing
- 4 oz (115g) cream cheese, softened
- 4 oz (115g) goat cheese or Boursin cheese, softened
- 1 tablespoon fresh dill, chopped (plus more for garnish)
- 1 tablespoon fresh lemon juice
- Salt and pepper, to taste
- 4-6 oz (115-170g) smoked salmon, thinly sliced
- Capers, for garnish (optional)

Instructions:

1. **Prepare the Crostini:**
   - Preheat the oven to 375°F (190°C). Place the baguette slices on a baking sheet and brush both sides lightly with olive oil. Bake for 8-10 minutes, flipping halfway through, until crisp and lightly golden. Remove from the oven and let cool.
2. **Prepare the Cheese Spread:**
   - In a small bowl, combine the softened cream cheese, goat cheese (or Boursin cheese), chopped fresh dill, lemon juice, salt, and pepper. Mix until smooth and well combined.
3. **Assemble the Crostini:**
   - Spread a layer of the cheese mixture onto each cooled baguette slice.
4. **Add Smoked Salmon:**
   - Top each crostini with a slice of smoked salmon, folding or layering it attractively.
5. **Garnish:**
   - Garnish the crostini with additional fresh dill and capers, if desired.
6. **Serve:**
   - Arrange the smoked salmon crostini on a serving platter and serve immediately.

Tips:

- To add a bit of freshness, you can also top each crostini with a small squeeze of fresh lemon juice just before serving.
- You can prepare the cheese spread and toast the baguette slices ahead of time, but assemble the crostini just before serving to keep them crisp.
- If you prefer, you can substitute the goat cheese or Boursin cheese with cream cheese mixed with a bit of sour cream for a lighter texture.

Enjoy these Smoked Salmon Crostini as a delightful appetizer that's perfect for any gathering or special occasion!

Buffalo Cauliflower Bites

Ingredients:

- 1 head of cauliflower, cut into florets
- 1/2 cup all-purpose flour (or chickpea flour for a gluten-free option)
- 1/2 cup water
- 1 teaspoon garlic powder
- 1 teaspoon paprika
- 1/2 teaspoon salt
- 1/4 teaspoon black pepper
- 1 tablespoon unsalted butter, melted (or olive oil)
- 1/2 cup buffalo hot sauce (such as Frank's RedHot or your favorite brand)
- Optional for serving: ranch or blue cheese dressing, celery sticks

Instructions:

1. **Preheat the Oven:**
   - Preheat your oven to 450°F (230°C). Line a baking sheet with parchment paper or lightly grease it.
2. **Prepare the Cauliflower:**
   - Wash the cauliflower thoroughly and cut it into bite-sized florets.
3. **Prepare the Batter:**
   - In a large bowl, whisk together the flour, water, garlic powder, paprika, salt, and pepper until smooth and well combined.
4. **Coat the Cauliflower:**
   - Toss the cauliflower florets in the batter until evenly coated, shaking off any excess batter.
5. **Bake the Cauliflower:**
   - Arrange the coated cauliflower florets in a single layer on the prepared baking sheet.
   - Bake for 20-25 minutes, flipping halfway through, until the cauliflower is golden brown and crispy.
6. **Make the Buffalo Sauce:**
   - In a separate bowl, mix together the melted butter and buffalo hot sauce until well combined.
7. **Toss the Cauliflower in Buffalo Sauce:**
   - Once the cauliflower florets are done baking, transfer them to a large bowl.
   - Pour the buffalo sauce mixture over the cauliflower and toss gently until all florets are coated evenly.
8. **Serve:**
   - Transfer the buffalo cauliflower bites to a serving platter.
   - Serve immediately with ranch or blue cheese dressing on the side for dipping, and celery sticks if desired.

Tips:

- Adjust the amount of buffalo hot sauce according to your spice preference. You can also mix in a bit of honey or maple syrup for a touch of sweetness to balance the heat.
- For extra crispy cauliflower, you can spray or drizzle the coated florets with olive oil before baking.
- These buffalo cauliflower bites are best served immediately to maintain their crispiness, but you can store leftovers in an airtight container in the refrigerator for up to 2 days. Reheat in the oven to crisp them up again before serving.

Enjoy these Buffalo Cauliflower Bites as a flavorful and satisfying appetizer or snack!

Mozzarella Stick

Ingredients:

- 1 head of cauliflower, cut into florets
- 1/2 cup all-purpose flour (or chickpea flour for a gluten-free option)
- 1/2 cup water
- 1 teaspoon garlic powder
- 1 teaspoon paprika
- 1/2 teaspoon salt
- 1/4 teaspoon black pepper
- 1 tablespoon unsalted butter, melted (or olive oil)
- 1/2 cup buffalo hot sauce (such as Frank's RedHot or your favorite brand)
- Optional for serving: ranch or blue cheese dressing, celery sticks

Instructions:

1. **Preheat the Oven:**
   - Preheat your oven to 450°F (230°C). Line a baking sheet with parchment paper or lightly grease it.
2. **Prepare the Cauliflower:**
   - Wash the cauliflower thoroughly and cut it into bite-sized florets.
3. **Prepare the Batter:**
   - In a large bowl, whisk together the flour, water, garlic powder, paprika, salt, and pepper until smooth and well combined.
4. **Coat the Cauliflower:**
   - Toss the cauliflower florets in the batter until evenly coated, shaking off any excess batter.
5. **Bake the Cauliflower:**
   - Arrange the coated cauliflower florets in a single layer on the prepared baking sheet.
   - Bake for 20-25 minutes, flipping halfway through, until the cauliflower is golden brown and crispy.
6. **Make the Buffalo Sauce:**
   - In a separate bowl, mix together the melted butter and buffalo hot sauce until well combined.
7. **Toss the Cauliflower in Buffalo Sauce:**
   - Once the cauliflower florets are done baking, transfer them to a large bowl.
   - Pour the buffalo sauce mixture over the cauliflower and toss gently until all florets are coated evenly.
8. **Serve:**
   - Transfer the buffalo cauliflower bites to a serving platter.
   - Serve immediately with ranch or blue cheese dressing on the side for dipping, and celery sticks if desired.

Tips:

- Adjust the amount of buffalo hot sauce according to your spice preference. You can also mix in a bit of honey or maple syrup for a touch of sweetness to balance the heat.
- For extra crispy cauliflower, you can spray or drizzle the coated florets with olive oil before baking.
- These buffalo cauliflower bites are best served immediately to maintain their crispiness, but you can store leftovers in an airtight container in the refrigerator for up to 2 days. Reheat in the oven to crisp them up again before serving.

Enjoy these Buffalo Cauliflower Bites as a flavorful and satisfying appetizer or snack!

Mozzarella Stick

Ingredients:

- 12 mozzarella string cheese sticks
- 1 cup all-purpose flour
- 2 large eggs, beaten
- 1 cup Italian-style breadcrumbs (or panko breadcrumbs)
- 1/2 cup grated Parmesan cheese
- 1 teaspoon dried oregano
- 1 teaspoon dried basil
- 1/2 teaspoon garlic powder
- 1/2 teaspoon onion powder
- Salt and pepper, to taste
- Oil, for frying (vegetable or canola oil)
- Marinara sauce, for dipping

Instructions:

1. **Prepare the Breading Station:**
    - In three separate shallow bowls or dishes, prepare the following:
        - Bowl 1: All-purpose flour
        - Bowl 2: Beaten eggs
        - Bowl 3: Italian-style breadcrumbs mixed with grated Parmesan cheese, dried oregano, dried basil, garlic powder, onion powder, salt, and pepper.
2. **Coat the Mozzarella Sticks:**
    - Remove the mozzarella sticks from their packaging and cut them in half to make 24 shorter sticks.
    - Dip each mozzarella stick into the flour, shaking off any excess.
    - Dip it into the beaten eggs, allowing any excess to drip off.
    - Roll it in the breadcrumb mixture, pressing gently to coat it evenly. Repeat the egg and breadcrumb coating process for a thicker crust, if desired.
    - Place the coated mozzarella sticks on a baking sheet lined with parchment paper. Freeze them for at least 30 minutes to help set the breading.
3. **Fry the Mozzarella Sticks:**
    - Heat oil in a deep fryer or large pot to 350°F (175°C).
    - Carefully place a few mozzarella sticks into the hot oil, making sure not to overcrowd the pan. Fry in batches for about 1-2 minutes, or until golden brown and crispy.
    - Remove the fried mozzarella sticks with a slotted spoon and place them on a plate lined with paper towels to drain excess oil.
4. **Serve:**
    - Serve the mozzarella sticks hot with marinara sauce for dipping.

Tips:

- Freezing the breaded mozzarella sticks before frying helps them retain their shape and prevents the cheese from melting too quickly.
- If you prefer a healthier option, you can bake the breaded mozzarella sticks in a preheated oven at 400°F (200°C) for about 8-10 minutes, turning halfway through, until golden brown and crispy.
- Serve these mozzarella sticks as a delicious appetizer or snack for parties, game days, or any occasion where you want to impress with homemade cheesy goodness!

Enjoy making and indulging in these crispy and gooey mozzarella sticks!

Greek Salad Skewers

Ingredients:

- Cherry or grape tomatoes
- Cucumber, cut into chunks
- Kalamata olives, pitted
- Feta cheese, cut into cubes
- Red onion, cut into wedges and separated
- Greek salad dressing (homemade or store-bought)
- Wooden skewers

Instructions:

1. **Prepare Ingredients:**
   - Wash and dry the cherry or grape tomatoes.
   - Peel and cut the cucumber into chunks.
   - Pit the Kalamata olives if necessary.
   - Cut the feta cheese into cubes.
   - Cut the red onion into wedges and separate the layers.
2. **Assemble the Skewers:**
   - Thread the ingredients onto wooden skewers in a desired pattern. For example, you can start with a cherry tomato, followed by a piece of cucumber, a cube of feta cheese, a Kalamata olive, and a wedge of red onion. Repeat the pattern until the skewer is filled, leaving some space at both ends for easy handling.
3. **Drizzle with Dressing:**
   - Arrange the assembled Greek Salad Skewers on a serving platter.
   - Drizzle the skewers with Greek salad dressing just before serving, or serve the dressing on the side for dipping.
4. **Serve:**
   - Serve the Greek Salad Skewers immediately as a colorful and flavorful appetizer.

Tips:

- Customize the skewers with additional ingredients such as bell peppers, artichoke hearts, or even grilled chicken or shrimp for added protein.
- If using wooden skewers, soak them in water for about 30 minutes before threading to prevent them from burning during grilling or broiling.
- These skewers can be prepared ahead of time and stored covered in the refrigerator until ready to serve. Drizzle with dressing just before serving to keep them fresh and crisp.

Enjoy these refreshing and delicious Greek Salad Skewers as a perfect appetizer for parties, gatherings, or any occasion!

Sushi Rolls

Ingredients:

- Sushi rice (1 cup uncooked rice makes about 3 rolls)
- Nori sheets (seaweed sheets)
- Sushi vinegar (rice vinegar mixed with sugar and salt)
- Fillings of your choice:
    - Sliced raw fish (such as salmon, tuna)
    - Cooked seafood (such as shrimp, crab)
    - Vegetables (such as cucumber, avocado, carrots)
    - Cream cheese, if desired
    - Sesame seeds, for garnish
    - Soy sauce, for serving
    - Pickled ginger and wasabi, for serving (optional)

Equipment Needed:

- Bamboo sushi rolling mat (makisu)
- Plastic wrap (optional)
- Sharp knife

Instructions:

1. **Prepare the Sushi Rice:**
    - Rinse the sushi rice under cold water until the water runs clear to remove excess starch.
    - Cook the rice according to the package instructions or in a rice cooker with the appropriate amount of water.
    - While the rice is still hot, transfer it to a large bowl and gently fold in the sushi vinegar (2 tablespoons rice vinegar, 1 tablespoon sugar, 1 teaspoon salt, mixed together and cooled). Mix gently to coat the rice evenly and let it cool to room temperature.
2. **Prepare the Fillings:**
    - Prepare your chosen fillings by slicing them into thin strips or pieces that will fit neatly inside the sushi rolls.
3. **Assemble the Sushi Rolls:**
    - Place a bamboo sushi rolling mat on a flat surface. If desired, cover it with plastic wrap to prevent the rice from sticking.
    - Lay a sheet of nori (shiny side down) on the bamboo mat.
    - Moisten your hands with water to prevent the rice from sticking. Spread a thin, even layer of sushi rice over the nori, leaving about 1 inch of nori uncovered at the top edge.
4. **Add the Fillings:**

- Arrange your fillings horizontally across the center of the rice-covered nori sheet.
5. **Roll the Sushi:**
   - Lift the edge of the bamboo mat closest to you, using your fingers to hold the fillings in place. Roll the bamboo mat away from you, pressing gently but firmly to shape the roll.
   - Continue rolling until you reach the uncovered edge of the nori. Wet the edge with a bit of water to seal the roll.
6. **Slice the Sushi:**
   - Use a sharp knife to slice the sushi roll into bite-sized pieces. Dip the knife in water between cuts to keep it from sticking to the rice.
7. **Serve:**
   - Arrange the sushi rolls on a plate and garnish with sesame seeds if desired.
   - Serve with soy sauce, pickled ginger, and wasabi on the side.

Tips:

- Experiment with different fillings and combinations to create your favorite sushi rolls.
- Use a sushi rolling mat (makisu) to help shape the rolls evenly and tightly.
- For inside-out rolls (uramaki), start with the rice on the outside and the nori on the inside. You can sprinkle sesame seeds or roe on the rice before rolling.
- Enjoy your homemade sushi rolls fresh, as they are best consumed soon after making.

Making sushi rolls at home allows you to customize the fillings and flavors to your liking, providing a delicious and satisfying meal or appetizer experience!

Prosciutto-Wrapped Asparagus

Ingredients:

- 1 bunch of asparagus spears (about 1 lb or 450g), tough ends trimmed
- 6-8 slices of prosciutto, thinly sliced
- Olive oil, for drizzling
- Black pepper, freshly ground

Instructions:

1. **Preheat the Oven:**
    - Preheat your oven to 400°F (200°C).
2. **Prepare the Asparagus:**
    - Wash the asparagus spears and trim off the tough ends.
3. **Wrap with Prosciutto:**
    - Take a slice of prosciutto and cut it lengthwise into halves or thirds, depending on the length of the asparagus spears.
    - Wrap each asparagus spear tightly with a piece of prosciutto, starting from the bottom and wrapping towards the tip. Repeat with the remaining asparagus and prosciutto slices.
4. **Arrange on Baking Sheet:**
    - Place the prosciutto-wrapped asparagus spears in a single layer on a baking sheet lined with parchment paper.
5. **Drizzle with Olive Oil:**
    - Drizzle olive oil over the prosciutto-wrapped asparagus spears. This helps the prosciutto crisp up and adds flavor.
6. **Season with Pepper:**
    - Grind black pepper over the asparagus to taste.
7. **Bake:**
    - Bake in the preheated oven for about 10-15 minutes, or until the asparagus is tender and the prosciutto is crispy.
8. **Serve:**
    - Remove from the oven and let cool slightly before serving.
    - Arrange the prosciutto-wrapped asparagus on a serving platter and serve warm.

Tips:

- You can add a sprinkle of grated Parmesan cheese or a drizzle of balsamic glaze over the prosciutto-wrapped asparagus before baking for additional flavor.
- Serve these asparagus spears as an appetizer or a side dish for any occasion. They pair wonderfully with a glass of white wine.
- Feel free to adjust the cooking time based on the thickness of your asparagus spears. Thinner spears may cook faster, so keep an eye on them to prevent overcooking.

Enjoy these delicious prosciutto-wrapped asparagus spears as a tasty appetizer that is sure to impress your guests!

Chicken Empanadas

Ingredients:

For the dough:

- 2 cups all-purpose flour
- 1/2 teaspoon salt
- 1/2 cup cold unsalted butter, cut into cubes
- 1/4 - 1/2 cup ice water

For the filling:

- 1 tablespoon olive oil
- 1 small onion, finely chopped
- 2 cloves garlic, minced
- 1/2 red bell pepper, finely chopped
- 1/2 green bell pepper, finely chopped
- 1 teaspoon ground cumin
- 1/2 teaspoon paprika
- 1/2 teaspoon chili powder (adjust to taste)
- Salt and pepper to taste
- 2 cups cooked shredded chicken (rotisserie chicken works well)
- 1/2 cup frozen peas (optional)
- 1/4 cup chopped fresh cilantro or parsley
- Juice of 1/2 lime
- 1/2 cup shredded cheese (cheddar, Monterey Jack, or your choice)

Instructions:

1. **Make the dough:**
    - In a large bowl, whisk together the flour and salt.
    - Add the cold butter cubes and use your fingers or a pastry cutter to cut the butter into the flour until the mixture resembles coarse crumbs.
    - Gradually add the ice water, a little at a time, mixing with a fork until the dough comes together and forms a ball. You may not need all of the water.
    - Wrap the dough in plastic wrap and refrigerate for at least 30 minutes.
2. **Make the filling:**
    - Heat olive oil in a large skillet over medium heat. Add the onion and cook until softened, about 3-4 minutes.
    - Add the garlic, red bell pepper, and green bell pepper. Cook for another 3-4 minutes until the peppers are softened.
    - Stir in the cumin, paprika, chili powder, salt, and pepper. Cook for 1 minute until fragrant.

- Add the shredded chicken and peas (if using). Cook, stirring occasionally, for about 2-3 minutes until heated through.
- Remove from heat and stir in the chopped cilantro or parsley and lime juice. Let the filling cool slightly, then stir in the shredded cheese.

3. **Assemble the empanadas:**
    - Preheat your oven to 375°F (190°C). Line a baking sheet with parchment paper.
    - On a lightly floured surface, roll out the chilled dough to about 1/8 inch thickness. Using a round cutter or a bowl, cut out circles of dough (about 5-6 inches in diameter).
    - Place a spoonful of the chicken filling in the center of each dough circle. Fold the dough over the filling to create a half-moon shape. Press the edges together to seal, then crimp with a fork to ensure a tight seal.
4. **Bake the empanadas:**
    - Place the assembled empanadas on the prepared baking sheet. Brush the tops with beaten egg or milk for a golden finish (optional).
    - Bake for 20-25 minutes, or until the empanadas are golden brown and crispy.
5. **Serve:**
    - Remove from the oven and let cool slightly before serving. Enjoy your delicious homemade chicken empanadas!

Feel free to adjust the seasonings and ingredients to suit your taste. These empanadas can be served as an appetizer, snack, or even a main course alongside a salad or other sides.

Sweet Potato Fries

Ingredients:

- 2 large sweet potatoes, peeled (if desired) and cut into thin strips (about 1/4 inch wide)
- 2 tablespoons olive oil
- 1/2 teaspoon salt, or to taste
- 1/2 teaspoon paprika
- 1/4 teaspoon garlic powder
- 1/4 teaspoon onion powder
- 1/4 teaspoon ground black pepper
- Optional: 1/4 teaspoon cayenne pepper (for a spicy kick)

Instructions:

1. **Preheat the oven:**
    - Preheat your oven to 425°F (220°C). Line a baking sheet with parchment paper or foil for easy cleanup.
2. **Prepare the sweet potatoes:**
    - Peel the sweet potatoes if desired (you can leave the skin on for added texture and nutrients). Cut them into thin, even strips resembling French fries.
3. **Season the sweet potatoes:**
    - In a large bowl, toss the sweet potato strips with olive oil until evenly coated.
    - In a small bowl, mix together salt, paprika, garlic powder, onion powder, black pepper, and cayenne pepper (if using). Sprinkle this seasoning mixture over the sweet potatoes and toss again to coat evenly.
4. **Arrange on baking sheet:**
    - Spread the seasoned sweet potato fries in a single layer on the prepared baking sheet. Make sure they are not overlapping to ensure even cooking and crispiness.
5. **Bake the sweet potato fries:**
    - Bake in the preheated oven for 20-25 minutes, flipping halfway through with a spatula to ensure even cooking. Bake until the sweet potato fries are golden brown and crispy on the outside.
6. **Serve:**
    - Once baked to your desired crispness, remove from the oven and let cool slightly. Serve hot as a delicious and healthier alternative to traditional fries.

Tips:

- For extra crispiness, you can sprinkle a little cornstarch over the sweet potato strips along with the seasoning before tossing with olive oil.

- Feel free to adjust the seasonings according to your taste preferences. You can experiment with different spices like smoked paprika, cumin, or even cinnamon for a sweet twist.
- These sweet potato fries are great on their own or served with your favorite dipping sauces such as ketchup, aioli, or a yogurt-based dip.

Enjoy your homemade sweet potato fries as a tasty and nutritious side dish or snack!

Cheese-Stuffed Mini Bell Peppers

Ingredients:

- 12 mini bell peppers, assorted colors
- 8 oz cream cheese, softened
- 1/2 cup shredded cheddar cheese (or your favorite cheese blend)
- 1/4 cup grated Parmesan cheese
- 1/4 teaspoon garlic powder
- 1/4 teaspoon onion powder
- 1/4 teaspoon paprika
- Salt and pepper to taste
- Optional: Chopped fresh herbs such as parsley or chives for garnish

Instructions:

1. **Prepare the mini bell peppers:**
   - Preheat your oven to 375°F (190°C). Line a baking sheet with parchment paper.
2. **Prepare the filling:**
   - In a mixing bowl, combine the softened cream cheese, shredded cheddar cheese, grated Parmesan cheese, garlic powder, onion powder, paprika, salt, and pepper. Mix until smooth and well combined.
3. **Stuff the mini bell peppers:**
   - Cut the tops off the mini bell peppers and carefully remove any seeds and membranes.
   - Spoon the cheese mixture into each pepper, filling them until just slightly overflowing.
4. **Bake the stuffed peppers:**
   - Place the stuffed mini bell peppers on the prepared baking sheet.
   - Bake in the preheated oven for 15-20 minutes, or until the peppers are tender and the cheese filling is melted and lightly golden on top.
5. **Serve:**
   - Remove from the oven and let cool slightly before serving. Optionally, garnish with chopped fresh herbs like parsley or chives.

Tips:

- If you like a bit of spice, you can add a pinch of cayenne pepper or red pepper flakes to the cheese mixture.
- Experiment with different cheeses such as mozzarella, Gruyère, or goat cheese for varied flavors.
- These cheese-stuffed mini bell peppers can be served warm or at room temperature. They make a great appetizer for parties or a delicious snack any time of day.

Enjoy these cheese-stuffed mini bell peppers as a tasty and colorful addition to your table!

Falafel Balls

Ingredients:

- 1 cup dried chickpeas (garbanzo beans), soaked overnight in water
- 1 small onion, roughly chopped
- 3 cloves garlic, minced
- 1/2 cup fresh parsley, chopped
- 1/2 cup fresh cilantro, chopped
- 1 teaspoon ground cumin
- 1 teaspoon ground coriander
- 1/4 teaspoon cayenne pepper (optional, for heat)
- 1 teaspoon salt, or to taste
- 1/2 teaspoon baking soda
- 2 tablespoons all-purpose flour or chickpea flour (besan), if needed
- Vegetable oil for frying

Instructions:

1. **Prepare the chickpeas:**
   - Drain and rinse the soaked chickpeas. Place them in a food processor.
2. **Blend the mixture:**
   - Add the chopped onion, minced garlic, parsley, cilantro, ground cumin, ground coriander, cayenne pepper (if using), salt, and baking soda to the food processor with the chickpeas.
   - Pulse the mixture until it forms a coarse paste. Scrape down the sides of the food processor as needed.
3. **Check the consistency:**
   - The mixture should be coarse and grainy but should hold together when pressed. If it's too wet, add 1-2 tablespoons of flour (all-purpose or chickpea flour) to help bind the mixture.
4. **Shape the falafel balls:**
   - Using your hands, shape the falafel mixture into small balls, about 1-1.5 inches in diameter. You should get about 20-24 falafel balls from this amount of mixture.
5. **Fry the falafel:**
   - Heat vegetable oil in a deep skillet or pot over medium-high heat, enough to submerge the falafel balls.
   - Carefully add the falafel balls in batches to the hot oil, frying for about 3-4 minutes per batch, or until they are golden brown and crispy. Use a slotted spoon to remove them from the oil and place them on a paper towel-lined plate to drain excess oil.
6. **Serve:**
   - Serve the falafel balls warm with pita bread, hummus, tahini sauce, chopped tomatoes, cucumbers, and lettuce.

Tips:

- **Baking option:** If you prefer baking instead of frying, preheat your oven to 375°F (190°C). Place the shaped falafel balls on a baking sheet lined with parchment paper. Brush them lightly with olive oil and bake for 20-25 minutes, flipping halfway through, until they are golden brown and crispy.
- **Make ahead:** You can prepare the falafel mixture ahead of time and refrigerate it until ready to use. Shape and fry (or bake) the falafel balls just before serving for the best texture.

Enjoy making and savoring these homemade falafel balls!

Stuffed Cherry Tomatoes

Ingredients:

- 24 cherry tomatoes
- 4 oz cream cheese, softened
- 2 tablespoons mayonnaise
- 1/4 cup finely shredded cheddar cheese (or your favorite cheese)
- 2 tablespoons finely chopped green onions or chives
- 1/4 teaspoon garlic powder
- Salt and pepper to taste
- Fresh herbs for garnish (optional)

Instructions:

1. **Prepare the cherry tomatoes:**
   - Wash the cherry tomatoes and pat them dry. Cut off the top of each tomato and scoop out the seeds and pulp using a small spoon or melon baller. You want to create a little cavity in each tomato for the filling.
2. **Make the filling:**
   - In a mixing bowl, combine the softened cream cheese, mayonnaise, shredded cheddar cheese, chopped green onions or chives, garlic powder, salt, and pepper. Mix until smooth and well combined.
3. **Fill the cherry tomatoes:**
   - Spoon or pipe the cheese mixture into each hollowed-out cherry tomato, filling them until slightly overflowing.
4. **Garnish and serve:**
   - Arrange the stuffed cherry tomatoes on a serving platter. If desired, garnish with fresh herbs like parsley or chives for added color and flavor.
5. **Chill and serve:**
   - Refrigerate the stuffed cherry tomatoes for at least 30 minutes to allow the flavors to meld together and the filling to set slightly before serving.

Tips:

- **Variations:** Feel free to customize the filling with other ingredients such as finely chopped bacon, diced bell peppers, or different herbs and spices.
- **Presentation:** For a festive touch, choose a variety of cherry tomato colors (red, yellow, and orange) to make the dish even more visually appealing.
- **Make ahead:** You can prepare the filling and hollow out the cherry tomatoes ahead of time. Fill them just before serving to ensure they stay fresh and crispy.

These stuffed cherry tomatoes are sure to be a hit at any gathering with their creamy and flavorful filling!

Beef Sliders

Ingredients:

- 1 pound ground beef (preferably 80% lean)
- Salt and pepper, to taste
- 1 teaspoon garlic powder
- 1 teaspoon onion powder
- 1/2 teaspoon smoked paprika (optional)
- 12 slider buns
- Your choice of toppings (lettuce, tomato slices, cheese, pickles, etc.)
- Condiments (ketchup, mustard, mayo, etc.)

Instructions:

1. **Prepare the beef patties:**
    - In a large bowl, combine the ground beef with salt, pepper, garlic powder, onion powder, and smoked paprika (if using). Mix gently with your hands until the seasonings are evenly distributed.
2. **Shape the sliders:**
    - Divide the seasoned beef mixture into 12 equal portions. Roll each portion into a ball and then flatten gently to form a small patty that is slightly wider than your slider buns (they will shrink a bit during cooking).
3. **Cook the sliders:**
    - Heat a skillet or grill pan over medium-high heat. Cook the sliders for about 3-4 minutes per side, or until they reach your desired level of doneness (medium-rare to medium is recommended for juicy sliders).
    - If using cheese, place a slice on each patty during the last minute of cooking and cover the skillet briefly to melt the cheese.
4. **Toast the slider buns:**
    - While the sliders are cooking, split the slider buns and lightly toast them on a separate skillet or grill until golden brown.
5. **Assemble the sliders:**
    - Place each cooked slider patty on the bottom half of a slider bun.
    - Add your desired toppings such as lettuce, tomato slices, pickles, etc.
6. **Serve:**
    - Close each slider with the top half of the bun and secure with toothpicks if needed. Arrange the sliders on a serving platter and serve immediately with your favorite condiments on the side.

Tips:

- **Variations:** Feel free to customize your sliders with different cheeses (cheddar, Swiss, blue cheese), sauces (barbecue sauce, aioli), or toppings (caramelized onions, sautéed mushrooms).
- **Make ahead:** You can prepare the beef patties ahead of time and refrigerate them until ready to cook. This makes it easier to handle during parties or gatherings.
- **Mini burgers:** If you don't have slider buns, you can use dinner rolls or small soft dinner rolls sliced in half.

These beef sliders are sure to be a crowd-pleaser with their juicy, flavorful patties and variety of customizable toppings!

Crab Rangoon

Ingredients:

- 8 oz cream cheese, softened
- 1 can (6 oz) lump crab meat, drained and flaked (or use imitation crab meat)
- 2 green onions, finely chopped
- 1 clove garlic, minced
- 1 teaspoon soy sauce
- 1/2 teaspoon Worcestershire sauce
- 1/4 teaspoon sesame oil
- 1/4 teaspoon ground ginger
- Salt and pepper, to taste
- 24-30 wonton wrappers
- Vegetable oil, for frying
- Sweet and sour sauce or sweet chili sauce, for dipping

Instructions:

1. **Prepare the filling:**
    - In a mixing bowl, combine the softened cream cheese, flaked crab meat, chopped green onions, minced garlic, soy sauce, Worcestershire sauce, sesame oil, ground ginger, salt, and pepper. Mix until well combined.
2. **Assemble the Crab Rangoon:**
    - Lay out a wonton wrapper on a clean surface. Place about 1 teaspoon of the crab and cream cheese mixture in the center of the wrapper.
3. **Shape the Crab Rangoon:**
    - Moisten the edges of the wonton wrapper with water using your fingertip. Fold the wrapper diagonally to form a triangle, pressing the edges firmly to seal. You can also fold the edges over each other to create a pouch-like shape or simply leave them as triangles.
4. **Fry the Crab Rangoon:**
    - Heat vegetable oil in a deep skillet or pot to about 350°F (175°C).
    - Carefully add the Crab Rangoon in batches, frying for about 2-3 minutes per batch, or until they are golden brown and crispy. Use a slotted spoon to remove them from the oil and place them on a paper towel-lined plate to drain excess oil.
5. **Serve:**
    - Serve the Crab Rangoon hot with sweet and sour sauce or sweet chili sauce for dipping.

Tips:

- **Baking option:** If you prefer a healthier option, you can bake the Crab Rangoon. Preheat your oven to 375°F (190°C). Arrange the filled wontons on a baking sheet lined

with parchment paper. Lightly spray or brush them with oil. Bake for about 12-15 minutes, or until they are crispy and golden brown.
- **Make ahead:** You can prepare the Crab Rangoon ahead of time and refrigerate them until ready to fry or bake. This makes it convenient for parties or gatherings.

Enjoy making and serving these homemade Crab Rangoon as a delicious appetizer!

Mini Tacos

Ingredients:

- Mini taco shells (store-bought or homemade)
- 1 pound ground beef or ground turkey
- 1 tablespoon olive oil
- 1 small onion, finely chopped
- 2 cloves garlic, minced
- 1 tablespoon taco seasoning (store-bought or homemade)
- Salt and pepper, to taste
- Toppings:
  - Shredded lettuce
  - Diced tomatoes
  - Shredded cheese (cheddar, Monterey Jack, or Mexican blend)
  - Sour cream
  - Salsa
  - Guacamole
  - Chopped cilantro (optional)
  - Lime wedges (for garnish)

Instructions:

1. **Prepare the mini taco shells:**
   - If using store-bought mini taco shells, follow the instructions on the package to heat them up or crisp them in the oven. If making homemade mini taco shells, you can use small tortillas and shape them into mini taco shells using a muffin tin or a taco rack. Bake them until they are crispy and hold their shape.
2. **Cook the ground meat:**
   - Heat olive oil in a skillet over medium-high heat. Add the chopped onion and cook until softened, about 3-4 minutes.
   - Add the minced garlic and cook for another 1 minute until fragrant.
   - Add the ground beef or turkey to the skillet, breaking it up with a spatula. Cook until browned and cooked through, about 5-7 minutes.
3. **Season the meat:**
   - Stir in the taco seasoning, salt, and pepper to taste. Cook for another 1-2 minutes, stirring to coat the meat evenly with the seasoning. Remove from heat.
4. **Assemble the mini tacos:**
   - Spoon a small amount of the seasoned meat into each mini taco shell.
5. **Add toppings:**
   - Top each mini taco with shredded lettuce, diced tomatoes, shredded cheese, sour cream, salsa, guacamole, and any other toppings you like.
6. **Serve:**

- Arrange the mini tacos on a serving platter. Garnish with chopped cilantro and lime wedges if desired. Serve immediately and enjoy!

Tips:

- **Variations:** You can customize the filling by using shredded chicken, pulled pork, or even vegetarian options like black beans or sautéed vegetables.
- **Make ahead:** Prepare the taco meat and toppings ahead of time, and assemble the mini tacos just before serving to keep the shells crispy.
- **Presentation:** Serve the mini tacos with a variety of toppings in separate bowls so guests can customize their tacos to their liking.

These mini tacos are sure to be a hit at parties or as a fun family meal option! Adjust the toppings and fillings to suit your taste preferences and enjoy the delicious flavors of homemade mini tacos.

Onion Rings

Ingredients:

- 2 large onions (yellow or white)
- 1 cup all-purpose flour
- 1 teaspoon baking powder
- 1 teaspoon salt
- 1/2 teaspoon black pepper
- 1 cup buttermilk (or regular milk)
- 1 egg
- Vegetable oil, for frying

Instructions:

1. **Prepare the onions:**
    - Peel the onions and slice them into 1/2-inch thick rings. Separate the rings and discard the smaller inner rings or save them for another use.
2. **Prepare the batter:**
    - In a mixing bowl, whisk together the flour, baking powder, salt, and black pepper.
    - In another bowl, whisk together the buttermilk (or regular milk) and egg until well combined.
3. **Coat the onion rings:**
    - Dip each onion ring into the flour mixture, shaking off any excess.
    - Then dip the floured ring into the buttermilk mixture, allowing any excess to drip off.
    - Dip the ring back into the flour mixture for a second coating. This double coating ensures a crispy texture.
4. **Fry the onion rings:**
    - Heat vegetable oil in a deep skillet or pot to about 350°F (175°C).
    - Carefully add a few onion rings to the hot oil, making sure not to overcrowd the pan. Fry in batches for about 2-3 minutes per side, or until they are golden brown and crispy.
    - Use a slotted spoon or tongs to transfer the fried onion rings to a paper towel-lined plate to drain excess oil. Season lightly with additional salt while still hot.
5. **Serve:**
    - Serve the onion rings hot and crispy as a side dish or appetizer. They pair well with dipping sauces like ketchup, ranch dressing, or a spicy aioli.

Tips:

- **Variations:** You can add different seasonings to the flour mixture such as garlic powder, smoked paprika, or cayenne pepper for a spicy kick.

- **Oven-baked option:** For a healthier alternative, you can bake the onion rings instead of frying them. Preheat your oven to 425°F (220°C). Arrange the coated onion rings on a baking sheet lined with parchment paper. Lightly spray or brush them with oil. Bake for about 15-20 minutes, flipping halfway through, until they are crispy and golden brown.
- **Make ahead:** You can prepare the onion rings up to the frying step ahead of time. Store the coated rings on a baking sheet lined with parchment paper in the refrigerator until ready to fry.

Enjoy making and savoring these crispy homemade onion rings!

BBQ Chicken Skewers

Ingredients:

- 1.5 lbs boneless, skinless chicken breasts or thighs, cut into 1-inch cubes
- 1 cup BBQ sauce (homemade or store-bought), plus extra for brushing
- 2 tablespoons olive oil
- 1 tablespoon soy sauce
- 1 tablespoon honey
- 1 teaspoon smoked paprika
- 1/2 teaspoon garlic powder
- 1/2 teaspoon onion powder
- Salt and pepper, to taste
- Wooden or metal skewers (if using wooden skewers, soak them in water for 30 minutes before using)

Instructions:

1. **Prepare the marinade:**
   - In a bowl, whisk together the BBQ sauce, olive oil, soy sauce, honey, smoked paprika, garlic powder, onion powder, salt, and pepper.
2. **Marinate the chicken:**
   - Place the chicken cubes in a resealable plastic bag or shallow dish. Pour half of the marinade over the chicken, reserving the other half for basting later. Ensure the chicken is evenly coated. Marinate in the refrigerator for at least 30 minutes, or up to 4 hours for maximum flavor.
3. **Skewer the chicken:**
   - Preheat your grill to medium-high heat or preheat your broiler in the oven.
   - Thread the marinated chicken cubes onto skewers, leaving a little space between each piece.
4. **Grill or broil the skewers:**
   - If grilling: Place the skewers on the preheated grill. Cook for 5-7 minutes per side, or until the chicken is fully cooked through and has nice grill marks. Brush with reserved marinade while grilling.
   - If broiling: Arrange the skewers on a lined baking sheet. Broil on high for about 5-7 minutes per side, or until the chicken is cooked through and slightly charred.
5. **Serve:**
   - Once cooked, remove the BBQ chicken skewers from the grill or oven. Brush with a little extra BBQ sauce if desired. Let them rest for a few minutes before serving.
6. **Garnish and enjoy:**
   - Serve the BBQ chicken skewers hot, garnished with chopped parsley or green onions if desired. They pair well with rice, salad, or grilled vegetables.

Tips:

- **Vegetable variation:** You can add chunks of bell peppers, onions, or cherry tomatoes between the chicken pieces on the skewers for added flavor and color.
- **Make ahead:** You can marinate the chicken ahead of time and keep it in the refrigerator until ready to grill or broil.
- **Safety note:** Ensure the chicken is cooked to an internal temperature of 165°F (74°C) to ensure it is fully cooked and safe to eat.

These BBQ chicken skewers are sure to be a hit at your next barbecue or family meal with their smoky, sweet, and tangy flavors!

Fried Calamari

Ingredients:

- 1 lb squid (calamari), cleaned and tubes cut into 1/2-inch rings
- 1 cup buttermilk (or regular milk)
- 1 cup all-purpose flour
- 1 teaspoon salt
- 1/2 teaspoon black pepper
- 1/2 teaspoon paprika
- Vegetable oil, for frying
- Lemon wedges, for serving
- Marinara sauce or aioli, for dipping

Instructions:

1. **Prepare the squid:**
   - Rinse the squid under cold water and pat dry with paper towels. Remove the tentacles if desired and cut the tubes into rings about 1/2-inch thick.
2. **Tenderize the squid (optional):**
   - If the squid is tough, you can tenderize it by pounding it lightly with a meat mallet or the back of a heavy knife. This step helps to ensure tender calamari after frying.
3. **Marinate the squid:**
   - Place the squid rings and tentacles (if using) in a bowl and pour buttermilk over them. Let them marinate for about 30 minutes to 1 hour. This step helps to tenderize the squid further and adds flavor.
4. **Prepare the breading:**
   - In a shallow dish or bowl, mix together the flour, salt, black pepper, and paprika.
5. **Bread the calamari:**
   - Heat vegetable oil in a deep fryer or large skillet to 350°F (175°C).
   - Remove the squid from the buttermilk, allowing any excess to drip off.
   - Dredge the squid rings and tentacles in the seasoned flour mixture, shaking off any excess.
6. **Fry the calamari:**
   - Carefully add a few pieces of calamari at a time to the hot oil, making sure not to overcrowd the pan. Fry for about 2-3 minutes, or until golden brown and crispy.
   - Use a slotted spoon or tongs to transfer the fried calamari to a paper towel-lined plate to drain excess oil. Sprinkle lightly with salt while still hot.
7. **Serve:**
   - Arrange the fried calamari on a serving platter. Serve hot with lemon wedges and your choice of marinara sauce or aioli for dipping.

Tips:

- **Garnish:** Garnish the fried calamari with chopped parsley or a squeeze of fresh lemon juice for extra flavor.
- **Variations:** You can add extra seasoning to the flour mixture such as garlic powder, onion powder, or cayenne pepper for a spicy kick.
- **Make ahead:** Fry the calamari just before serving for the best crispy texture. However, you can prepare the squid and dredge in flour ahead of time and keep it refrigerated until ready to fry.

Enjoy making and savoring these crispy and delicious homemade fried calamari as a delightful appetizer or main dish!

Artichoke Dip Stuffed Bread

Ingredients:

- 1 large loaf of Italian bread or French baguette
- 1 can (14 oz) artichoke hearts, drained and chopped
- 1 cup grated Parmesan cheese
- 1 cup shredded mozzarella cheese
- 1/2 cup mayonnaise
- 1/2 cup sour cream or Greek yogurt
- 2 cloves garlic, minced
- 1/4 teaspoon salt
- 1/4 teaspoon black pepper
- 1/4 teaspoon red pepper flakes (optional, for a bit of heat)
- 2 tablespoons chopped fresh parsley or chives, for garnish

Instructions:

1. **Prepare the bread:**
    - Preheat your oven to 375°F (190°C).
    - Cut the loaf of bread in half lengthwise. Scoop out some of the soft bread from the center of each half to create a hollowed-out space for the filling. Reserve the bread crumbs for another use or discard.
2. **Make the artichoke dip filling:**
    - In a mixing bowl, combine the chopped artichoke hearts, grated Parmesan cheese, shredded mozzarella cheese, mayonnaise, sour cream or Greek yogurt, minced garlic, salt, black pepper, and red pepper flakes (if using). Mix well until all ingredients are thoroughly combined.
3. **Fill the bread:**
    - Spread the artichoke dip mixture evenly into the hollowed-out halves of the bread.
4. **Bake the stuffed bread:**
    - Place the filled bread halves on a baking sheet lined with parchment paper or aluminum foil.
    - Bake in the preheated oven for about 20-25 minutes, or until the cheese is melted and bubbly, and the bread edges are golden brown.
5. **Serve:**
    - Remove from the oven and let cool slightly. Sprinkle with chopped fresh parsley or chives for garnish.
    - Slice the stuffed bread into pieces and serve warm as a delicious appetizer or snack.

Tips:

- **Variations:** You can add chopped spinach, sun-dried tomatoes, or cooked bacon to the artichoke dip mixture for additional flavors.
- **Presentation:** Serve the stuffed bread with additional dipping sauces like marinara sauce or a garlic aioli on the side.
- **Make ahead:** Prepare the artichoke dip filling ahead of time and store it in the refrigerator. Fill the bread and bake just before serving for a fresh and hot appetizer.

This artichoke dip stuffed bread is sure to be a hit at any gathering with its creamy, cheesy goodness and crispy bread exterior!

Spring Rolls

Ingredients:

- Rice paper wrappers (also known as spring roll wrappers)
- 1 cup cooked shrimp, peeled, deveined, and halved lengthwise
- 1 cup cooked vermicelli noodles (rice noodles), cooled
- 1 cup shredded lettuce or mixed salad greens
- 1 cup julienned cucumber
- 1 cup julienned carrots
- Fresh herbs (such as mint, cilantro, and Thai basil)
- Optional: Thinly sliced avocado, mango, or bell peppers for added flavor and color

Dipping Sauce:

- 1/4 cup hoisin sauce
- 2 tablespoons peanut butter
- 1 tablespoon soy sauce
- 1 tablespoon lime juice
- 1-2 tablespoons water, as needed to thin the sauce

Instructions:

1. **Prepare the filling ingredients:**
   - Cook the vermicelli noodles according to package instructions, rinse with cold water, and set aside to cool.
   - Prepare all vegetables and herbs by washing, peeling, and cutting them into thin strips or julienne.
2. **Prepare the dipping sauce:**
   - In a small bowl, whisk together hoisin sauce, peanut butter, soy sauce, lime juice, and water until smooth. Adjust the consistency with more water if needed. Set aside.
3. **Assemble the spring rolls:**
   - Fill a shallow dish or large bowl with warm water. Dip one rice paper wrapper into the water for about 5-10 seconds until it becomes soft and pliable (but still slightly firm).
   - Lay the softened rice paper wrapper flat on a clean work surface, such as a cutting board or a clean kitchen towel.
4. **Add the fillings:**
   - Place a small handful of lettuce or mixed greens on the bottom third of the rice paper wrapper, leaving about 1-2 inches of space from the edge.
   - Arrange a small portion of noodles, shrimp, cucumber, carrots, herbs, and any additional fillings you desire on top of the lettuce.
5. **Roll the spring roll:**

- Fold the bottom edge of the rice paper wrapper over the fillings, tucking it underneath.
- Fold in the sides of the wrapper over the filling. Continue to roll tightly from the bottom to the top, sealing the roll.

6. **Serve:**
   - Repeat with the remaining ingredients to make more spring rolls.
   - Serve the spring rolls whole or sliced in half on a serving platter with the dipping sauce on the side.

Tips:

- **Variations:** You can customize the fillings based on your preference. Try adding cooked chicken, tofu, avocado, mango slices, bean sprouts, or bell peppers.
- **Make ahead:** You can prepare the fillings and dipping sauce ahead of time. Assemble the spring rolls just before serving to keep the rice paper wrappers fresh and moist.
- **Storage:** If you need to store leftover spring rolls, wrap them individually in plastic wrap or store them in an airtight container in the refrigerator. They are best eaten fresh but can be stored for a day or two.

Enjoy these fresh and flavorful Vietnamese-style spring rolls as a healthy appetizer, light meal, or party snack!

Loaded Potato Skins

Ingredients:

- 4 large russet potatoes, scrubbed clean
- 2 tablespoons olive oil
- Salt and pepper, to taste
- 1 cup shredded cheddar cheese
- 4 slices cooked bacon, crumbled
- 2 green onions, thinly sliced
- Sour cream, for serving
- Chopped fresh parsley or chives, for garnish

Instructions:

1. **Preheat the oven:**
   - Preheat your oven to 400°F (200°C).
2. **Prepare the potatoes:**
   - Pierce each potato several times with a fork. Rub them with olive oil and sprinkle with salt and pepper.
   - Place the potatoes directly on the oven rack and bake for about 45-60 minutes, or until they are tender and can be easily pierced with a fork.
3. **Prepare the potato skins:**
   - Remove the potatoes from the oven and let them cool slightly until they are safe to handle. Leave the oven on.
   - Cut each potato in half lengthwise. Scoop out most of the flesh, leaving about 1/4 inch of potato attached to the skin. Reserve the scooped-out potato flesh for another use (like mashed potatoes).
4. **Bake the potato skins:**
   - Place the hollowed-out potato skins on a baking sheet lined with parchment paper.
   - Brush the insides of the potato skins with a little more olive oil. Season with additional salt and pepper if desired.
   - Bake in the oven for about 10 minutes, or until the skins are crispy and lightly browned.
5. **Fill the potato skins:**
   - Remove the potato skins from the oven. Sprinkle each skin with shredded cheddar cheese and crumbled bacon.
6. **Bake again:**
   - Return the filled potato skins to the oven and bake for another 5-7 minutes, or until the cheese is melted and bubbly.
7. **Serve:**
   - Remove from the oven and sprinkle with sliced green onions. Serve the loaded potato skins hot, with dollops of sour cream on top.

- Garnish with chopped fresh parsley or chives for added freshness and color.

Tips:

- **Variations:** You can customize the toppings based on your preferences. Add diced cooked chicken, sautéed mushrooms, or jalapeños for a spicy kick.
- **Make ahead:** You can bake the potato skins and prepare the toppings ahead of time. Fill and bake them just before serving to ensure they are hot and crispy.
- **Presentation:** Arrange the loaded potato skins on a serving platter and serve them as an appetizer or party snack.

These loaded potato skins are sure to be a crowd-pleaser with their crispy texture, gooey cheese, and savory toppings. Enjoy making and savoring them at your next gathering!

Avocado Toast Bites

Ingredients:

- 1 ripe avocado
- 1 small lemon or lime, juiced
- Salt and pepper, to taste
- 1-2 small tomatoes, diced
- 1/4 cup red onion, finely chopped
- 1 tablespoon chopped fresh cilantro or parsley (optional)
- 1-2 tablespoons crumbled feta cheese or goat cheese (optional)
- Slices of bread (whole grain, sourdough, or any bread of your choice)
- Olive oil, for drizzling
- Optional toppings: sliced radishes, microgreens, sesame seeds, balsamic glaze

Instructions:

1. **Prepare the avocado mixture:**
    - Cut the avocado in half, remove the pit, and scoop the flesh into a bowl.
    - Mash the avocado with a fork until smooth but still slightly chunky.
    - Stir in the lemon or lime juice to prevent the avocado from browning. Season with salt and pepper to taste.
2. **Prepare the toppings:**
    - In a separate bowl, combine the diced tomatoes, finely chopped red onion, and chopped cilantro or parsley. Season with a pinch of salt and pepper. Set aside.
3. **Toast the bread:**
    - Toast the slices of bread until golden brown and crispy. You can toast them in a toaster, toaster oven, or under the broiler.
4. **Assemble the avocado toast bites:**
    - Spread a generous layer of the mashed avocado onto each slice of toasted bread.
5. **Add toppings:**
    - Spoon the tomato and onion mixture evenly over the avocado on each toast bite.
    - Optionally, sprinkle with crumbled feta cheese or goat cheese for added flavor.
6. **Drizzle with olive oil and garnish:**
    - Drizzle a little olive oil over the avocado toast bites.
    - Garnish with additional toppings such as sliced radishes, microgreens, sesame seeds, or a drizzle of balsamic glaze for extra flavor and presentation.
7. **Serve:**
    - Arrange the avocado toast bites on a serving platter. Serve immediately as a delicious appetizer or snack.

Tips:

- **Variations:** Experiment with different toppings based on your preferences. Try adding cooked and crumbled bacon, sliced hard-boiled eggs, or a sprinkle of chili flakes for a spicy kick.
- **Make ahead:** Prepare the avocado mixture and toppings ahead of time. Assemble the avocado toast bites just before serving to keep the bread crispy.
- **Gluten-free option:** Use gluten-free bread if needed, and adjust toppings accordingly.

These avocado toast bites are not only delicious and nutritious but also easy to customize and perfect for any occasion, from brunch to parties!

Bruschetta with Fig and Goat Cheese

Ingredients:

- 1 French baguette, sliced into 1/2-inch thick rounds
- Olive oil, for brushing
- 8 oz goat cheese, softened
- 6-8 fresh figs, sliced (mission figs or any ripe variety)
- Honey, for drizzling
- Balsamic glaze, for drizzling (optional)
- Fresh thyme leaves, for garnish
- Salt and pepper, to taste

Instructions:

1. **Prepare the baguette slices:**
    - Preheat your oven to 375°F (190°C).
    - Arrange the baguette slices on a baking sheet. Brush both sides lightly with olive oil.
    - Bake in the preheated oven for about 8-10 minutes, or until the bread slices are golden and crispy. Remove from the oven and let them cool slightly.
2. **Assemble the bruschetta:**
    - Spread a layer of softened goat cheese onto each toasted baguette slice.
3. **Add figs:**
    - Place 1-2 slices of fresh fig on top of the goat cheese on each bruschetta slice.
4. **Drizzle with honey and balsamic glaze:**
    - Drizzle a little honey over each bruschetta slice with fig and goat cheese.
    - Optionally, drizzle a small amount of balsamic glaze over the top for added flavor.
5. **Season and garnish:**
    - Sprinkle a pinch of salt and pepper over the bruschetta slices.
    - Garnish each slice with fresh thyme leaves for a pop of color and additional flavor.
6. **Serve:**
    - Arrange the fig and goat cheese bruschetta on a serving platter. Serve immediately as an elegant appetizer.

Tips:

- **Variations:** You can add a few arugula leaves or a sprinkle of chopped walnuts for added texture and flavor.
- **Make ahead:** Prepare the toasted baguette slices and assemble the bruschetta components (goat cheese and figs) ahead of time. Assemble just before serving to keep the bread crispy.

- **Presentation:** Drizzle the honey and balsamic glaze in a decorative pattern over the bruschetta for an eye-catching presentation.

This bruschetta with fig and goat cheese is sure to impress with its combination of sweet figs, creamy goat cheese, and crunchy bread—a perfect appetizer for gatherings or special occasions!

Baked Brie with Jam

Ingredients:

- 1 wheel of Brie cheese (8-10 oz)
- 1/4 cup jam or fruit preserves (such as raspberry, apricot, fig, or your favorite)
- 1/4 cup chopped nuts (such as almonds, walnuts, or pecans)
- Fresh herbs, for garnish (optional)
- Crackers, sliced baguette, or apple slices, for serving

Instructions:

1. **Preheat the oven:**
   - Preheat your oven to 350°F (175°C).
2. **Prepare the Brie:**
   - Remove any packaging from the Brie cheese. Leave the rind on; it becomes soft and edible when baked.
   - Place the Brie wheel on a parchment paper-lined baking sheet or in a small oven-safe dish.
3. **Add the jam:**
   - Spread the jam or fruit preserves evenly over the top of the Brie cheese.
4. **Top with nuts:**
   - Sprinkle the chopped nuts over the jam-covered Brie cheese. This adds a nice crunch and additional flavor.
5. **Bake the Brie:**
   - Bake the Brie in the preheated oven for about 10-15 minutes, or until the cheese is soft and gooey inside. The time may vary depending on the size and thickness of the Brie wheel.
6. **Serve:**
   - Carefully transfer the baked Brie to a serving platter. Garnish with fresh herbs if desired.
   - Serve warm with crackers, sliced baguette, or apple slices for dipping and spreading.

Tips:

- **Variations:** Experiment with different types of jams or preserves to create unique flavor combinations. You can also try adding a drizzle of honey or a sprinkle of dried fruits like cranberries or apricots.
- **Presentation:** Serve the baked Brie with a cheese knife or spreader alongside the crackers or bread for easy serving.
- **Make ahead:** You can prepare the Brie with jam and nuts ahead of time and refrigerate it until ready to bake. Just bake it right before serving to ensure it's warm and gooey.

This baked Brie with jam makes a stunning and delicious appetizer for parties, gatherings, or special occasions. The combination of warm, melty cheese with sweet jam and crunchy nuts is sure to be a hit!

Teriyaki Beef Skewers

Ingredients:

- 1.5 lbs beef sirloin or flank steak, cut into 1-inch cubes
- Wooden or metal skewers (if using wooden skewers, soak them in water for 30 minutes)
- Sesame seeds and sliced green onions, for garnish (optional)

For the Teriyaki Marinade:

- 1/2 cup soy sauce
- 1/4 cup mirin (Japanese sweet rice wine)
- 1/4 cup brown sugar
- 2 tablespoons rice vinegar
- 2 cloves garlic, minced
- 1 teaspoon fresh ginger, grated
- 1 tablespoon cornstarch (optional, for thickening)

Instructions:

1. **Prepare the marinade:**
   - In a small saucepan, combine soy sauce, mirin, brown sugar, rice vinegar, minced garlic, and grated ginger. Bring to a simmer over medium heat, stirring occasionally.
   - If you prefer a thicker sauce, mix 1 tablespoon of cornstarch with 1 tablespoon of water to create a slurry. Add the slurry to the simmering sauce, stirring constantly until the sauce thickens slightly. Remove from heat and let it cool completely.
2. **Marinate the beef:**
   - Place the beef cubes in a bowl or resealable plastic bag. Pour half of the teriyaki marinade over the beef, reserving the other half for basting later. Ensure the beef is evenly coated. Marinate in the refrigerator for at least 30 minutes, or up to 4 hours for maximum flavor.
3. **Prepare the skewers:**
   - If using wooden skewers, thread the marinated beef cubes onto the skewers, leaving a little space between each piece.
4. **Grill or bake the skewers:**
   - Preheat your grill to medium-high heat or preheat your oven to 400°F (200°C).
   - If grilling: Place the skewers on the preheated grill. Cook for about 3-4 minutes per side, or until the beef is cooked to your desired doneness, basting occasionally with the reserved teriyaki marinade.
   - If baking: Place the skewers on a baking sheet lined with parchment paper or aluminum foil. Bake for about 10-12 minutes, turning once halfway through cooking, or until the beef is cooked through and caramelized.
5. **Serve:**

- Remove the teriyaki beef skewers from the grill or oven. Sprinkle with sesame seeds and sliced green onions for garnish if desired.
- Serve hot with steamed rice, stir-fried vegetables, or a side of salad.

Tips:

- **Vegetarian option:** You can substitute tofu or vegetables like bell peppers, mushrooms, and onions for a vegetarian version of teriyaki skewers.
- **Make ahead:** Prepare the teriyaki marinade and marinate the beef ahead of time. Skewer and cook just before serving for the best flavor and texture.
- **Safety note:** Ensure the beef reaches an internal temperature of at least 145°F (63°C) for medium-rare to medium doneness.

These teriyaki beef skewers are sure to be a hit with their tender, flavorful meat and deliciously sticky teriyaki glaze. Enjoy making and savoring them at your next barbecue or family dinner!

Chicken Quesadillas

Ingredients:

- 2 boneless, skinless chicken breasts, cooked and shredded (about 2 cups shredded chicken)
- 1 cup shredded cheese (Mexican blend, cheddar, or Monterey Jack)
- 4 large flour tortillas
- 1/2 cup diced bell peppers (any color)
- 1/2 cup diced onion
- 1 teaspoon chili powder
- 1/2 teaspoon cumin
- 1/2 teaspoon paprika
- Salt and pepper, to taste
- Cooking oil or butter, for cooking

Optional toppings:

- Salsa
- Sour cream
- Guacamole
- Chopped cilantro
- Lime wedges

Instructions:

1. **Prepare the filling:**
    - Heat a skillet over medium heat. Add a little oil and sauté the diced bell peppers and onion until softened, about 5-7 minutes.
    - Add the shredded chicken to the skillet along with chili powder, cumin, paprika, salt, and pepper. Stir well to combine and cook for another 2-3 minutes until heated through. Remove from heat and set aside.
2. **Assemble the quesadillas:**
    - Heat a large skillet or griddle over medium heat.
    - Place one tortilla on the skillet. Spread an even layer of shredded cheese over half of the tortilla.
    - Spoon a generous portion of the chicken and vegetable mixture over the cheese.
    - Fold the tortilla over to cover the filling, creating a half-moon shape. Press down gently with a spatula.
3. **Cook the quesadillas:**
    - Cook the quesadilla for about 2-3 minutes on each side, or until golden brown and crispy, and the cheese is melted.
    - Repeat with the remaining tortillas and filling.
4. **Serve:**

- Remove the quesadillas from the skillet and place them on a cutting board. Let them cool for a minute, then slice each quesadilla into wedges.
- Serve hot with salsa, sour cream, guacamole, chopped cilantro, and lime wedges on the side for dipping.

Tips:

- **Variations:** Add sliced jalapeños, black beans, corn kernels, or diced tomatoes to the filling for extra flavor and texture.
- **Make ahead:** Prepare the chicken filling ahead of time and store it in the refrigerator. Assemble and cook the quesadillas just before serving to ensure they are hot and crispy.
- **Gluten-free option:** Use gluten-free tortillas if needed.
- **Customize:** Feel free to adjust the seasoning and cheese type according to your taste preferences.

These chicken quesadillas are perfect for a quick weeknight dinner or as a crowd-pleasing appetizer at parties. Enjoy making and serving them with your favorite toppings!

Greek Spanakopita

Ingredients:

- 1 pound (450g) fresh spinach, washed and chopped (or 10 ounces frozen spinach, thawed and squeezed dry)
- 1/2 cup chopped green onions or finely chopped onion
- 2 tablespoons chopped fresh dill (or 2 teaspoons dried dill)
- 1/4 cup chopped fresh parsley
- 1 cup crumbled feta cheese
- 1/2 cup ricotta cheese or cottage cheese
- 3 eggs, lightly beaten
- Salt and pepper, to taste
- 1/4 teaspoon ground nutmeg (optional)
- 1/4 cup olive oil, plus more for brushing phyllo sheets
- 1/2 pound (about 20 sheets) phyllo pastry sheets, thawed if frozen
- Butter, melted (optional)

Instructions:

1. **Prepare the filling:**
   - If using fresh spinach, wash thoroughly and chop. If using frozen spinach, thaw completely and squeeze out excess water.
   - In a large mixing bowl, combine the spinach, green onions (or onion), dill, parsley, feta cheese, ricotta or cottage cheese, beaten eggs, salt, pepper, and nutmeg (if using). Mix well to combine.
2. **Prepare the phyllo pastry:**
   - Preheat your oven to 350°F (175°C).
   - Unwrap the phyllo pastry sheets and cover them with a damp towel to prevent them from drying out while you work.
   - Brush a 9x13-inch baking dish with olive oil.
3. **Assemble the spanakopita:**
   - Lay one sheet of phyllo pastry in the prepared baking dish and brush it lightly with olive oil. Repeat with 9 more sheets, brushing each one with olive oil.
   - Spread half of the spinach and cheese mixture evenly over the layered phyllo sheets.
4. **Add another layer of phyllo:**
   - Layer 10 more sheets of phyllo pastry over the spinach mixture, brushing each sheet with olive oil as before.
   - Spread the remaining spinach and cheese mixture evenly over the second layer of phyllo.
5. **Finish with a top layer of phyllo:**
   - Layer the remaining phyllo sheets on top, again brushing each sheet with olive oil. If desired, brush the very top layer with melted butter for extra richness.

6. **Bake the spanakopita:**
    - Using a sharp knife, carefully score the top layer of phyllo into squares or diamonds (this will make it easier to cut after baking).
    - Bake in the preheated oven for 45-50 minutes, or until the top is golden brown and crispy.
7. **Serve:**
    - Remove from the oven and let cool for a few minutes before cutting into squares or triangles along the scored lines.
    - Serve warm or at room temperature. Spanakopita is delicious on its own or with a side of tzatziki sauce.

Tips:

- **Variations:** Add a squeeze of lemon juice or a pinch of lemon zest to the spinach mixture for a hint of brightness.
- **Make ahead:** You can assemble the spanakopita a few hours ahead of time and refrigerate it until ready to bake. Brush with olive oil or melted butter just before baking.
- **Storage:** Leftover spanakopita can be stored in an airtight container in the refrigerator for up to 3 days. Reheat in the oven to restore its crispiness.

Enjoy this delicious Greek spanakopita as a flavorful appetizer or as part of a Mediterranean-inspired meal!

Tomato Basil Crostini

Ingredients:

- 1 French baguette, sliced into 1/2-inch thick rounds
- Olive oil, for brushing
- 2 cups cherry tomatoes, halved
- 2 cloves garlic, minced
- 1/4 cup fresh basil leaves, thinly sliced (chiffonade)
- Balsamic glaze, for drizzling (optional)
- Salt and pepper, to taste

Instructions:

1. **Prepare the baguette slices:**
   - Preheat your oven to 375°F (190°C).
   - Arrange the baguette slices on a baking sheet. Brush both sides lightly with olive oil.
2. **Bake the baguette slices:**
   - Bake in the preheated oven for about 8-10 minutes, or until the bread slices are golden brown and crispy. Remove from the oven and let them cool slightly.
3. **Prepare the tomato topping:**
   - In a bowl, combine the halved cherry tomatoes, minced garlic, and thinly sliced basil leaves. Season with salt and pepper to taste. Toss gently to combine.
4. **Assemble the crostini:**
   - Top each toasted baguette slice with a spoonful of the tomato and basil mixture. Arrange them on a serving platter.
5. **Drizzle with balsamic glaze (optional):**
   - For an extra touch of flavor, drizzle a small amount of balsamic glaze over each crostini.
6. **Serve:**
   - Serve the tomato basil crostini immediately as an appetizer or snack.

Tips:

- **Variations:** You can add a sprinkle of crumbled feta cheese or shaved Parmesan cheese on top for added richness.
- **Make ahead:** You can prepare the tomato and basil topping ahead of time and store it in the refrigerator. Toast the baguette slices and assemble the crostini just before serving to keep them crispy.
- **Presentation:** Garnish with additional basil leaves or a twist of freshly ground black pepper for an attractive presentation.

This tomato basil crostini is perfect for serving at parties, gatherings, or as a starter to a meal. It's quick to make and bursts with fresh flavors that everyone will enjoy!

Coconut Shrimp

Ingredients:

- 1 pound large shrimp, peeled and deveined (tails left on or removed, based on preference)
- 1 cup all-purpose flour
- 1/2 teaspoon salt
- 1/4 teaspoon black pepper
- 2 large eggs, beaten
- 1 cup sweetened shredded coconut
- 1 cup panko breadcrumbs (or regular breadcrumbs)
- Oil for frying (vegetable oil or coconut oil)

Instructions:

1. **Prepare the shrimp:**
    - Pat the shrimp dry with paper towels to remove excess moisture.
2. **Set up the breading station:**
    - In one shallow dish, place the flour, salt, and pepper. Mix well.
    - In another shallow dish, place the beaten eggs.
    - In a third shallow dish, combine the shredded coconut and panko breadcrumbs.
3. **Coat the shrimp:**
    - Dip each shrimp first into the flour mixture, shaking off any excess.
    - Next, dip the shrimp into the beaten eggs, allowing any excess to drip off.
    - Finally, press the shrimp into the coconut and breadcrumb mixture, ensuring it is evenly coated on all sides. Press gently to adhere the coating.
4. **Heat the oil:**
    - In a large skillet or frying pan, heat about 1/2 inch of oil over medium-high heat until hot (around 350°F or 175°C).
5. **Fry the shrimp:**
    - Carefully place the coated shrimp in the hot oil, a few at a time, making sure not to overcrowd the pan. Fry for about 2-3 minutes per side, or until the shrimp are golden brown and crispy.
6. **Transfer and drain:**
    - Remove the fried shrimp from the oil using a slotted spoon or tongs and place them on a plate lined with paper towels to drain excess oil.
7. **Serve:**
    - Serve the coconut shrimp hot with your favorite dipping sauce, such as sweet chili sauce, mango salsa, or a creamy dip like aioli or tartar sauce.

Tips:

- **Baking option:** If you prefer a healthier option, you can bake the coconut shrimp. Preheat the oven to 400°F (200°C), place the breaded shrimp on a baking sheet lined with parchment paper, and lightly spray or brush them with oil. Bake for about 10-12 minutes, flipping halfway through, until golden and crispy.
- **Variations:** You can add a pinch of cayenne pepper or chili powder to the flour mixture for a spicy kick.
- **Make ahead:** You can bread the shrimp ahead of time and refrigerate them until ready to fry or bake.

Enjoy these crispy and flavorful coconut shrimp as a delicious appetizer or part of a seafood feast!

Pesto Pinwheels

Ingredients:

- 1 sheet of puff pastry, thawed (about 10x10 inches)
- 1/4 cup basil pesto (store-bought or homemade)
- 1/2 cup shredded mozzarella cheese (or any cheese of your choice)
- 1/4 cup grated Parmesan cheese
- Optional: 1/4 cup sun-dried tomatoes, chopped
- Optional: Fresh basil leaves, chopped, for garnish

Instructions:

1. **Preheat the oven:**
   - Preheat your oven to 400°F (200°C). Line a baking sheet with parchment paper or lightly grease it.
2. **Prepare the puff pastry:**
   - On a lightly floured surface, unfold the thawed puff pastry sheet. Roll it out slightly to smooth any creases and to make it a bit larger if needed.
3. **Spread pesto and cheese:**
   - Spread the basil pesto evenly over the puff pastry sheet, leaving a small border around the edges.
   - Sprinkle the shredded mozzarella cheese and grated Parmesan cheese evenly over the pesto.
   - If using, scatter the chopped sun-dried tomatoes over the cheese.
4. **Roll the pastry:**
   - Starting from one edge, tightly roll up the puff pastry sheet like a jelly roll or Swiss roll. Roll all the way to the opposite edge.
   - Place the seam side down and gently press the roll to seal.
5. **Slice into pinwheels:**
   - Using a sharp knife, slice the roll into 1/2 to 3/4-inch thick slices. You should get about 12-14 slices.
6. **Arrange on baking sheet:**
   - Place the pinwheels on the prepared baking sheet, spacing them slightly apart.
7. **Bake:**
   - Bake in the preheated oven for 15-18 minutes, or until the pinwheels are puffed and golden brown.
8. **Serve:**
   - Remove from the oven and let cool slightly on the baking sheet. Transfer to a serving platter.
   - Garnish with chopped fresh basil leaves if desired.
   - Serve warm as a delicious appetizer or snack.

Tips:

- **Variations:** Feel free to customize the filling with different types of cheese, such as goat cheese or feta, and add toppings like sliced olives or roasted red peppers.
- **Make ahead:** You can prepare the pesto pinwheels up to the slicing step, then cover and refrigerate them. Bake them just before serving to ensure they are fresh and crispy.
- **Freezing:** If you want to freeze them, place the sliced pinwheels on a baking sheet in a single layer and freeze until firm. Then transfer to a freezer bag or container. Bake from frozen, adding a few extra minutes to the baking time.

These pesto pinwheels are sure to be a hit with their savory pesto and cheese filling wrapped in flaky puff pastry. Enjoy making and sharing them with friends and family!

Crab-Stuffed Mushrooms

Ingredients:

- 24 large button mushrooms, cleaned with stems removed
- 8 oz lump crab meat, drained and picked over for shells
- 4 oz cream cheese, softened
- 1/4 cup mayonnaise
- 1/4 cup grated Parmesan cheese
- 2 green onions, finely chopped
- 1 clove garlic, minced
- 1 tablespoon fresh lemon juice
- 1/2 teaspoon Worcestershire sauce
- Salt and pepper, to taste
- 1/4 cup breadcrumbs (optional, for topping)
- Fresh parsley, chopped, for garnish

Instructions:

1. **Prepare the mushrooms:**
   - Preheat your oven to 350°F (175°C). Line a baking sheet with parchment paper.
   - Remove the stems from the mushrooms and discard (or reserve for another use). Place the mushroom caps on the prepared baking sheet.
2. **Prepare the filling:**
   - In a medium bowl, combine the lump crab meat, softened cream cheese, mayonnaise, grated Parmesan cheese, chopped green onions, minced garlic, lemon juice, Worcestershire sauce, salt, and pepper. Mix well until everything is thoroughly combined.
3. **Fill the mushrooms:**
   - Spoon a generous amount of the crab filling into each mushroom cap, filling them until slightly mounded.
4. **Optional breadcrumb topping:**
   - If desired, sprinkle a little breadcrumbs over the tops of the stuffed mushrooms for added crunch and texture.
5. **Bake the mushrooms:**
   - Bake in the preheated oven for 18-20 minutes, or until the mushrooms are tender and the filling is heated through and lightly golden on top.
6. **Garnish and serve:**
   - Remove from the oven and let cool for a few minutes. Garnish with chopped fresh parsley before serving.
7. **Serve warm:**
   - Arrange the crab-stuffed mushrooms on a serving platter and serve warm as an appetizer.

Tips:

- **Variations:** You can add additional ingredients to the filling such as diced bell peppers, a pinch of cayenne pepper for heat, or a sprinkle of Old Bay seasoning for a more seafood-inspired flavor.
- **Make ahead:** Prepare the stuffed mushrooms up to a day in advance and refrigerate them covered. Bake them just before serving to ensure they are fresh and hot.
- **Presentation:** For a decorative touch, sprinkle a little extra Parmesan cheese or paprika on top of the stuffed mushrooms before baking.

These crab-stuffed mushrooms are perfect for parties, holiday gatherings, or as a special appetizer for any occasion. They're sure to impress with their creamy, crab-filled goodness!

Mini Beef Wellingtons

Ingredients:

- 4 beef fillet steaks (about 6 oz each)
- Salt and pepper, to taste
- 2 tablespoons olive oil
- 8 oz mushrooms, finely chopped
- 2 cloves garlic, minced
- 2 tablespoons butter
- 1 tablespoon thyme leaves, chopped
- 1/4 cup dry white wine (optional)
- 1 sheet puff pastry, thawed if frozen
- 1 egg, beaten (for egg wash)

Instructions:

1. **Prepare the Beef:**
   - Season the beef fillets with salt and pepper on both sides.
   - Heat olive oil in a skillet over high heat. Sear the fillets for about 2 minutes on each side, until browned. Remove from heat and let cool.
2. **Make the Mushroom Duxelles:**
   - In the same skillet, melt butter over medium heat. Add mushrooms, garlic, and thyme. Cook, stirring frequently, until mushrooms release their moisture and become golden brown.
   - If using, add white wine to deglaze the pan. Cook until the wine evaporates. Remove from heat and let cool.
3. **Assemble the Wellingtons:**
   - Roll out the puff pastry on a lightly floured surface. Cut into squares large enough to wrap around each fillet.
   - Spread a layer of mushroom duxelles over each piece of puff pastry.
   - Place a seared fillet on top of the mushroom duxelles.
   - Wrap the pastry around the fillet, sealing the edges with egg wash.
4. **Bake:**
   - Preheat oven to 400°F (200°C).
   - Place the wrapped fillets seam side down on a baking sheet lined with parchment paper.
   - Brush the tops with egg wash.
   - Bake for 20-25 minutes, or until the pastry is golden brown and the beef reaches your desired level of doneness (medium rare is recommended for tender results).
5. **Serve:**
   - Let the Mini Beef Wellingtons rest for a few minutes before serving.
   - Optionally, garnish with additional thyme leaves or a drizzle of sauce.

These Mini Beef Wellingtons are perfect for parties or special occasions, offering a bite-sized version of the classic dish that's sure to impress your guests!

Stuffed Jalapeno Peppers

Ingredients:

- 12 jalapeno peppers
- 8 oz cream cheese, softened
- 1 cup shredded cheddar cheese
- 1/2 teaspoon garlic powder
- 1/2 teaspoon onion powder
- 1/4 teaspoon paprika
- Salt and pepper, to taste
- 6 slices bacon, cooked and crumbled (optional)
- Fresh cilantro or parsley, chopped (for garnish)

Instructions:

1. **Prepare the Jalapenos:**
    - Preheat your oven to 400°F (200°C).
    - Cut the jalapeno peppers in half lengthwise. Remove the seeds and membranes. You can use a spoon to scrape them out.
2. **Make the Filling:**
    - In a mixing bowl, combine the softened cream cheese, shredded cheddar cheese, garlic powder, onion powder, paprika, salt, and pepper. Mix until well combined.
    - If using bacon, crumble it into small pieces and add it to the cheese mixture. Stir until evenly distributed.
3. **Stuff the Jalapenos:**
    - Spoon the cheese mixture into each jalapeno half, filling them evenly.
4. **Bake:**
    - Place the stuffed jalapenos on a baking sheet lined with parchment paper or aluminum foil.
    - Bake in the preheated oven for 15-20 minutes, or until the peppers are tender and the cheese is melted and slightly golden on top.
5. **Serve:**
    - Remove from the oven and let them cool slightly before serving.
    - Garnish with chopped fresh cilantro or parsley if desired.

These stuffed jalapeno peppers are spicy, creamy, and packed with flavor. They make a fantastic appetizer for any occasion and can be enjoyed hot or at room temperature. Adjust the filling ingredients to your taste preferences, adding more spices or herbs as desired.

Mediterranean Hummus Platter

Ingredients:

- Hummus (homemade or store-bought)
- Cherry tomatoes, halved
- Cucumber, sliced
- Kalamata olives
- Feta cheese, cubed or crumbled
- Red onion, thinly sliced
- Roasted red peppers, sliced
- Fresh parsley or mint, chopped
- Extra virgin olive oil
- Lemon wedges
- Pita bread or pita chips, for serving

Instructions:

1. **Prepare the Ingredients:**
   - If making homemade hummus, prepare it according to your favorite recipe or use a store-bought version.
2. **Arrange the Platter:**
   - Choose a large serving platter or board. Spread the hummus evenly over the center of the platter, creating a smooth surface.
3. **Decorate with Ingredients:**
   - Around the hummus, arrange the cherry tomatoes, cucumber slices, Kalamata olives, feta cheese cubes or crumbles, red onion slices, and roasted red pepper slices. Distribute them in an appealing pattern, alternating colors and textures.
4. **Garnish:**
   - Sprinkle the chopped fresh parsley or mint over the hummus and around the platter for a burst of freshness.
5. **Drizzle with Olive Oil and Lemon:**
   - Drizzle extra virgin olive oil over the hummus and some of the other ingredients on the platter. Squeeze lemon wedges over the hummus and around the platter for added brightness.
6. **Serve:**
   - Serve the Mediterranean Hummus Platter immediately with pita bread or pita chips on the side for dipping.

Tips:

- **Variations:** You can customize the platter with additional Mediterranean ingredients such as artichoke hearts, sun-dried tomatoes, or marinated mushrooms.

- **Make it Ahead:** Prepare components of the platter ahead of time and assemble just before serving to keep the ingredients fresh.
- **Accompaniments:** Alongside pita bread or chips, you can also serve fresh vegetables like carrots or bell pepper strips for dipping.

This Mediterranean Hummus Platter is not only visually appealing but also offers a variety of flavors and textures that everyone will enjoy. It's perfect for parties, gatherings, or even as a light and satisfying lunch option.

www.ingramcontent.com/pod-product-compliance
Lightning Source LLC
LaVergne TN
LVHW062046070526
838201LV00080B/2107